Free To Love

Jordan and Margaret Paul

Published by Evolving Publications

Los Angeles

Originally published in hardcover by J.P. Tarcher, 1975
ISBN: 0-87477-036-X
Paperback edition by Pyramid Books, 1976
ISBN: 0-515-04080-0
Trade paperback edition by Evolving Publications, 1983
ISBN: 0-912389-00-1
Library of Congress Catalog Card Number: 74-27653
Printed in the United States of America
Published by Evolving Publications, 2531 Sawtelle Blvd. #42
Los Angeles, California 90064

Table of Contents

Pregnancy and Children

Responsibility and Equality

Control and Conflict

Secrets and Revelations

Affirmations and Freedom

Love and Intimacy

Foreword

This is not a book about marriage. It is a marriage.

Married couples don't usually share their relationship with others, but as marriage counselors we listen daily to what other couples have to say. We have seen how their rewards and difficulties are in large part similar to one another's and to our own, and have discovered how helpful it can be when we openly share our marital experiences with them. As we have found ways to work on our own conflicts and maintain our in-love feelings for each other, we believe we have found ways to help others do the same.

In this book we tell about the experiences and understandings that have happened over our eleven years of marriage. As we share our lives and what "free to love" means to us, we hope to open doorways to intimacy for any couple involved in a close, continuing relationship.

The focus of our book is intimacy. But rather than just talking about what intimacy is, we want to be intimate with you. Creating intimacy and sustaining it while working toward being free and independent people is the single greatest challenge of our relationship. Intimacy is not something we work toward and, once attained, have as a permanent possession. It requires continuing moments of intimacy built upon each other. Ours grows as much as we are willing to put in the time and effort, and for us, half the marriage is the working on it.

We are committed to making our marriage exciting and deeply satisfying. This commitment means we are willing to work to find ways through our difficult times. As counselors we are aware of how easy it is to leave a marriage or to find relationships outside of it which one hopes will bring relief from an unhappy situation. But a new relationship usually runs into the same problems which caused the breakup of the previous one, or into new equally disturbing difficulties. If we leave a difficult situation without understanding our part in it, we may never break through to awareness and self-acceptance. That breakthrough is the result of the intimacy which comes from commitment; a commitment which in turn grows with each breakthrough to intimacy.

The time we took to reach new awarenesses about ourselves as individuals and our relationship is often compressed in our stories. Frequently these awarenesses emerged only after weeks, months or sometimes years of living with situations that somehow did not seem right. We had chosen over and over again (most of the time unaware that we were making a choice) not to confront these situations openly. Eventually one of us would decide to express his or her feelings, and then we realized we had a specific problem to deal with. Once we became aware of a problem, we needed to talk and talk about it until we felt accepting of ourselves and of each other.

It is difficult for us to feel accepting of our own or another person's behavior when that behavior makes us unhappy. To be accepting does not necessarily mean changing our behavior or changing what we want. Acceptance requires a thorough understanding of the good reasons the other person has for doing what he does. If we can put ourselves into the other person's place and experience his reality without judging him, we can reach that state of deep understanding where love and intimacy flourish.

For focus we have divided our book into sections, although in life problems in one area cannot be isolated from difficulties in another. At the beginning of the book each section is essentially chronological, but toward the end it is less structured as our revelations and affirmations about marriage expanded, deepened and became far more complex.

The problems we discuss are our problems and all of them will certainly not apply to every couple. For example, our marriage does not have many of the areas of contention that we often encounter in counseling— especially in relation to child-raising, religion, social issues, and moral attitudes. Although we are very different in temperament, our basic views on these matters are similar, and we have included such broad issues only when they directly affected the intimacy of our relationship.

We are not suggesting that anyone pattern their marriage after ours. Each couple develops a shape to their relationship which is individual to them, and this is as it should be for there is clearly no single "right form" into which a relationship should be molded. Just as ours is always changing as we go through new experiences and gain new awarenesses, so all living marriages are in a process of growth and transition. For ourselves and our readers, our hope is that this movement is toward intimacy—growing together, not growing apart.

Jordan and Margaret Paul
March, 1975

Courtship
and
Marriage

We Meet: We're Very Different

It all started with a phone call to my friend Roger.

"How come you never fixed me up with that girl you fixed Bob up with last night?" I said.

"Margie?"

"Yeah."

"She's not your type. I don't think you'd like her."

"Why not?"

"She's a scatterbrained artist. Her life is wild and weird. You're very different kinds of people."

"Well, give me her number anyway. What have I got to lose?"

"Hello, Margie? My name is Jordan Paul. Roger gave me your number."

Oh no! Not another of Roger's jerky friends. A college fraternity type, no doubt. Boring.

For the two years since my divorce Roger had been fixing me up with his friends. The guys were all the same. Their one interest was getting me into bed.

"Hi," I said, wondering how I was going to turn him down without hurting his feelings.

"Roger said we might like each other. How about getting together for coffee?"

Oh well, an hour for coffee couldn't be too bad. What do I have to lose?

"What do you do?" I asked, hoping he was somewhat stable and at least did something interesting.

"I'm collecting unemployment."

Wow. A real loser. Oh well, it's only an hour.

Jordan walked in—tall, dark, and handsome.

"Hi," I said, smiling. He certainly was beautiful.

"Ah-choo," he answered. "Do you have cats? I'm allergic to cats."

"Yeah, I have two."

"Let's get out of here."

Already he doesn't like my cats.

We talked a lot about ourselves. He asked me something no one else ever had: What was I reading? He even listened to the answers.

What a night! She's the first girl in years I could really talk to. She's exciting. Roger's right, we're very different. And those cats have got to go.

That wasn't half bad. In fact, I really enjoyed myself. He seems to be an open person, and I like that. Most of the guys I've met don't seem to know what a feeling is. I wonder why he didn't try to get me into bed like all of Roger's other friends? He sure is different. He didn't even try to kiss me. Maybe it was my cats.

It's Magic

We spent our second date relaxing at Jordan's apartment, just talking and getting to know each other. On our third date we went to a party a friend of mine was giving. Since we didn't know many people there, Jordan and I spent the evening talking to each other.

Suddenly, as we were laughing at the same thing, our eyes really met. We kissed.

For a divorced lady who had kissed more than one guy, my reaction was intense and unexpected. All I remember about the rest of the party is that I couldn't stop smiling.

We went back to Jordan's apartment. It had taken him a while to get started, but once he got going he sure didn't waste time! I pulled back. Enough for one night.

I've Never Had An Orgasm

By our fourth date, I knew we were headed for something special. No more holding back. I decided to tell Jordan about my sexual problem before we had intercourse.

I had never had an orgasm with a man. After two years of my first marriage, I had gone into intensive psychoanalysis to deal with this and other problems, but four years later I still hadn't succeeded in attaining that coveted orgasm.

By this time, after all those years of analysis, it wasn't a difficult thing for me to talk about. I had not, however, told many of the men I had been involved with. It seemed risky to talk about my problem with a person I cared about. I wanted to be accepted and approved of, and I was afraid that most men wouldn't understand. So, whenever I made love I said nothing and just pretended to have an orgasm. I would end up feeling bad about the whole experience. I didn't want that to happen this time. As we were holding each other and talking about our feelings, I took a deep breath and said, "I've never had an orgasm with a man."

There was a pause, and I waited apprehensively for his response. "You haven't?" He seemed unsure.

"No, I don't know why but I just can't."

"Maybe I don't know what I'm getting into," he answered, "but I feel that somehow it will be all right."

That evening we talked a lot about what I'd been through with my sexuality. After that I never wanted to pretend. Taking the risk and being open with Jordan was one of the best things I ever did for our relationship.

I'll Help Her If I Can, But Can I?

I never knew very much about the sexuality of any woman I'd been involved with. I'd never talked directly to a woman about her orgasm. Margie could have pretended with me, and I never would have known.

I wanted to help Margie with her problem, but right then I really wanted to get her into bed.

She's Tough, But Reasonable

"Tonight, I'm going to make dinner," I announced three weeks after we'd met.

"I'd love it," Margie said. "Let's do the shopping together."

I had already planned the menu—one of my special meal-in-itself salads. With Margie in tow I zipped to the salad dressing section and routinely put a bottle in the shopping cart. Margie took it out, put it back on the shelf and picked out another one, announcing, "This one is better for you."

"Wait a minute, that's my favorite salad dressing, and I don't even know if I'll like this one."

"Just read the labels. Your salad dressing is full of chemicals, and this one doesn't have any," she said.

Uh oh. I knew a health food nut when I saw one. My mother had always been concerned about eating the right foods. She wouldn't buy white bread, and we had liver once a week for dinner. A liver sandwich on whole wheat bread became the symbol of my fight against those who were out to deprive me of hot dogs and ice cream sodas. Now, after six years of freedom, I was face to face with another nut.

Margie and I stalled in front of the salad dressings. "I don't believe in any of that stuff," I said, putting her bottle back and recovering my original choice.

We moved on. I took a loaf of bread from the shelf.

"That bread is awful," she said.

"I love it."

"Do you know what they put in white bread?" I don't remember answering that question, but she went on anyway. "A lot of chemicals. They take out all of the nutrition and substitute chemicals."

She was adamant now. Even more aggravating, she seemed to know what she was talking about. I felt my salad dressing and white bread slipping away.

"Okay," I said, "I'm not going to argue with you. I'll make you a deal. I'll go along with your food nuttiness, but I will not eat anything that I don't like, just because it's good for me."

"That's fine with me, but promise me one thing," she said.

"What's that?"

"That you'll read a book that I'll give you so that you can learn something about food."

"It's a deal."

Margie was tough but reasonable. We could disagree and still get along. We were on our way.

I hope she hates liver.

I Don't Know What She Sees In Me

We had just seen *Who's Afraid of Virginia Woolf.* Margie had suggested we go in the first place, and we weren't even out of the theater before she was bubbling about how exciting it was.

"The whole play was just two sick people yelling at each other," I said. "I fell asleep in the second act."

"How could you fall asleep?"

Tension mounted as we got into the car. Margie got so much meaning from the play. I didn't. She had so much to say about it, and I didn't understand it at all.

As we drove home in silence I thought about how different our reactions had been. She's intelligent and insightful. Maybe I'm not. I like musical comedies, and novels and nonfiction—things that are straightforward and easy to understand. Margie likes to discuss abstract art, movies and plays that are heavy with symbolism, and impossibly intellectual books. I never liked those kinds of things and always put them down with my standard response: "That's dumb."

We had reacted so differently. I wondered what Margie saw in me.

What If He Doesn't Like The Things I Like?

What a frustrating evening.

Maybe he was tired.

Maybe he had other things on his mind.

Maybe he was upset over something.

How could he fall asleep during Virginia Woolf? What's the matter with him? That's the kind of play I love to get into and discuss, and he falls asleep. I'm so disappointed.

But I feel that he's sensitive and intelligent. Maybe he doesn't think that he is.

What if he doesn't like the things I like?

I think I love him. There's got to be a way . . .

I've Got To Know What's Happening

I excitedly drove over to Jordan's apartment to show him my new haircut. I hoped he would like it.

Although we had known each other for less than six weeks, and despite our obvious differences, Jordan had become very, very important to me. I had already begun to think about marrying him.

He was standing outside as I pulled up. I jumped out of the car and ran smiling up to him. He looked right through me.

"What's the matter—don't you like my haircut?"

"Huh? Oh, yeah. Sure. It's fine."

"Well, what's wrong, then?"

"What makes you think something's wrong?"

"You don't seem very happy to see me." *Oh god! Is he losing interest in me? What's happening? He's probably decided that he doesn't want to be too involved. Maybe it's the orgasm thing.*

When I'm scared or anxious, I have to do something about it. Well, I was scared. I had to find out what was going on.

"Hey, I need to talk to you," I said.

We went into his apartment and sat on his bed.

"Look, I know something's not right, and it's really scaring me."

"No, really. Everything's fine."

"Then why the distant greeting?"

"I wasn't distant."

"Oh, come on. You're being distant right now! Are you scared to tell me that you want to call off our relationship?"

"No, no, it's nothing like that."

"Then what is it? Tell me!"

"Oh shit. Well, what happened is that, well, uh, this girl just called, and she thinks she's pregnant. I know she was screwing around with a lot of guys so it's probably not me, but she says it is. My involvement with her was superficial and now she is coming back to haunt me. Why does she pick on me instead of one of the others? Hell, it probably happened before we met."

"Why were you afraid to tell me that?"

"I guess I was afraid that you might decide that the situation was too complicated and would back out of our relationship."

"Well, I'm glad you told me. We'll work it out. I really got scared when you weren't glad to see me. Let's back up and start over. Do you like my hair?"

My First Orgasm

I was astounded! We were ecstatic!

My first orgasm with Jordan was a momentous occasion.

It took a long period of direct clitoral stimulation to bring me to orgasm, but that was just fine with both of us.

I realized soon after that why orgasm had been impossible in my relationships with other men. Never before had I felt the commitment and acceptance that we offered each other. Even though we had known each other for only two months, I had complete trust that Jordan would be there for me and I knew I wanted to be there for him. I hadn't known, before meeting Jordan, that my sexuality was so tied up with acceptance and commitment.

When I was finally able to commit myself totally, it was the beginning of my growth as a sexual person.

Valuing Emotions

I am a person who feels deeply, but I had always wanted to deny it and never let anyone know about it. I used to envy guys who were cool and uninvolved, and I had tried to make myself appear unemotional and aloof.

Margie didn't feel the way I did about emotions. When I cried in a movie that we saw together, I was embarrassed, but Margie told me that when she could see and hear my feelings, she felt warm and close to me.

"I know that you're a very emotional person and I love that part of you," she said. No one had ever told me that before, and I found it very hard to believe. I considered that side of me a liability and of no value. To Margie it was of ultimate value.

Having found a woman who valued me as an emotional person, I knew I couldn't let her go. For the first time in years, I began to think seriously about marriage.

We're Honest But It's Scary

We decided to live together.

Well, we didn't actually decide. I just stopped going home, except to feed my cats. Even though Jordan was unemployed and I was in school only in the morning, we never seemed to have enough time together. We spent hours talking every day and long into the night, letting each other in on our fears, our hopes and dreams. We were determined not to base this relationship on false images and half-truths. We had both experienced the disaster of that kind of involvement.

"There's something I want to tell you, but I'm scared that you'll be angry at me for not telling you earlier, before we got so involved," Jordan said.

I cuddled closer, waiting to hear, certain that I could accept almost anything he would tell me.

"Well," Jordan continued, "I told you I was married once before. That's not true. I have been married twice. My second marriage lasted only six months and was annulled How do you feel about being involved with a two-time loser?"

I felt relieved to know that another secret was shared. I hugged Jordan and reassured him that I was still willing to chance it.

Each day we revealed more of ourselves to each other. We talked of our childhood and our teen years, of our past marriages and what had happened to them, our other loves, and our disappointments. We talked about how we felt about each other, what we wanted from the other, and what frightened us about our new-found intimacy.

It was a time of great intensity and passion, and great honesty. At the end of four months we felt very close, very open, very vulnerable. We decided to get married.

Reprise: We're Very Different

He's content.	She's ambitious.
He's low-key.	She's high-strung.
He moves slowly.	She races.
He likes sports—period.	She loves potting, sewing, crafts, theatre, all kinds of education.
He believes he's intellectually inadequate.	She feels intellectually secure.
He thinks he's shallow.	She thinks she's deep.
He's socially adept.	She's ill-at-ease.
He's humorous.	She's serious.
He's a day person.	She's a night owl.

We got married.

Everyone said, "They're so different. Their marriage will never last."

Problems
and
Adjustments

Sitting And Watching

I was an addict.

I didn't take drugs, smoke or drink. I was hooked on watching sports on TV. Football, baseball, basketball— every game was "the game of the year," no matter who was playing whom or what.

For as long as I could remember, sports served important purposes in my life. When my life was unfulfilling and unexciting, watching the games provided a few thrills. It was even a way to let my emotions out if I wanted to. It was a socially acceptable and inexpensive way of filling countless hours. It gave me a lot to talk about.

And it was so easy. I didn't have to leave the comfort of my own home. It made no demands on me. Sitting "stoned" in front of the set, I didn't have to think about anything or relate to anyone.

Moving And Doing

"Stop rushing around so much," Jordan would yell at me as I whizzed past him. "What's the matter with you? Can't you ever relax? Come on, sit down a minute with me."

"No, I don't want to now."

From the beginning I had told Jordan that I needed some time for myself. As an only child, I had gotten used to being alone. Other children had their brothers and sisters around all the time. In the evenings I had no one so I learned how to be alone and feel okay about it. I developed many interests because I had to, and had grown accustomed to amusing myself.

I loved reading, sewing, sculpting and making pots. I played tennis and took classes. Being an active, high-energy person, I found it difficult to sit around and do nothing, or just watch television with Jordan, which is what he wanted to do.

When Jordan and I were courting, nothing seemed as important as just being together. Now that we were married, I found it difficult to spend long periods of time with him. I would get tense, anxious and nervous, and feel as if I needed to get away to do something productive, to accomplish something.

When I wanted time away from him, Jordan felt I didn't care about being with him, and was often hurt and angry. On the other hand, the amount of time that he spent sitting around not doing anything important bugged the hell out of me.

"How can you watch TV all the time," I'd say. "There's so much to do!"

Our differences were creating problems.

Going Our Separate Ways

"You're so goddamn busy all the time! Why be married if all these other things are so much more important to you than being with me?" Jordan yelled.

"These things are a hell of a lot more fun than watching TV," I yelled back. We'd been married for six months, and it was our third argument that week.

Jordan and I didn't spend much time together during the day anymore. I was in graduate school working on my master's in art education, and he was now working full time for his father learning to be a building contractor. At night he was glued to the TV, and I was busy studying or working on one of my crafts.

Jordan often tried to lure me away from what I was doing. Sometimes I would give in, and we'd sit on the couch and stare together.

By 11:30 we were tired, and we hadn't had any closeness all evening. We were so far apart emotionally that we found it hard to get involved with each other.

We both knew something was wrong, but we didn't see the pattern developing in our relationship. After several days of being distant, we would get into a pretty good fight. Usually it was over something trivial, but it created an involvement between us. When the argument was resolved, we would feel close enough to talk and make love.

Choosing the lifestyles we did made it difficult to sustain our intimacy. Being involved with projects meant that I had limited time, and because Jordan was so uninvolved he had little to offer when we were together. We had been creating conflicts to bridge the gap.

Instead of trying to understand and cope with each other's choices, we were putting each other down for being different.

Maybe they were right about our marriage not lasting.

There's So Much That I'm Missing

Even though Margie tried hard to join me in my
world of sports, she never really understood what was so
captivating about it. But she never pushed me to give up
my interest. If she had, I would have rebelled. Instead, I
started to watch her as she enjoyed her activities. She
seemed to get so much real satisfaction from all the
things she did. I felt jealous. Inadequate. I wanted to
share more with her, to share her knowledge, her
excitement and, most of all, her good feelings about
herself.

Risking Failure

Margie came right out and said it. "I'm very much in love with you, but I'm afraid that as I continue to learn and grow, we'll get further and further apart. I need you to grow with me and bring me some intellectual stimulation."

We had been married for one year. Margie, still working toward her master's degree, had just started teaching in high school. If I couldn't keep up with her, maybe I'd lose her.

"I don't even know where to start," I said.

"How about going back to school?"

School!

"The thought of going back to school terrifies me. I got very bad feelings about myself in school. I never felt that I understood as much as other people did, and I had to cheat a lot just to get through."

"I don't know what was going on then, but you're an intelligent person and I'm sure you'll do well now."

"You sound just like my mother. People have always told me that, but I've never believed them. Even though I may never fail, I am afraid I might."

"Besides, I don't even know what to take in school."

"What about getting a teaching credential in psychology, since that was your major?"

"You know, I've always thought I might like teaching but never seriously considered it. The pay is so bad. How can anybody be happy on a teacher's salary?"

"Look," Margie said, "I know that a lot of my happiness will depend on your being happy in what you're doing. Besides, I'm working too. We'll do okay."

Frightened and unsure, I started back to school. It didn't take me long to realize that I had changed during the seven years since my graduation from college. Learning was easier and more purposeful. I was in school because I wanted to be and I had a goal. As I dug into many issues, I became excited about education and about teaching.

The more I succeeded, the more I believed in myself. Margie was supportive. Our relationship was growing. I felt happy and alive.

I Like Myself Better

I was taking a course in improving writing skills. The professor told us to pick a play, read it and the reviews it had received and then write our own review. I chose *Who's Afraid of Virginia Woolf*. I got a recording, bought a copy of the play, and went home to listen and to read.

The play still seemed abstract, but I was determined to make sense out of it. I asked Margie to listen with me.

As I got to know George, Martha, Honey, and Nick, I felt that I understood why they behaved as they did. I read the reviews and listened a third, fourth, and fifth time. By the time I sat down to write my paper, I could see that the play brought out the difficulty of knowing what is truth in our lives and what is illusion. I could relate it to myself, and to Margie and me, and I felt a sense of excitement and pride.

When I had first seen it, I was defensive because I didn't understand it. This time I had worked at it until I understood. The better I knew the play, the better I liked it . . . and me.

Stuttering, The Bane Of My Existence

When people get nervous, it shows up in different ways. Some people get an ulcer or have high blood pressure. Others eat too much. Some break out in hives.

When I get nervous I stutter.

It started when I was three years old. My mother said that suddenly I could hardly get a word out.

In grammar school I was okay with my friends, but I had a terrible time talking or reading out loud in class. Speech therapy didn't help.

In junior high it was worse. I was humiliated when I had to stand in front of the class to give a report and I just couldn't speak. It's still a painful memory.

I suffered through high school, still afraid to open my mouth in class. I joined the drama class, though, and got a part. It was through sheer determination that I was able to act in a school play. The experience was agonizing.

I gave a speech at graduation. I can't remember whether I stuttered or not. I can only remember the terror that I felt beforehand.

Now I was student-teaching in a remedial reading class, and part of my job was to read aloud. Jordan worked with me hour after hour, helping me to relax. I'd read out loud to him and when I'd get so tense that the words wouldn't come out, he helped me to calm down. When I was able to benefit from his disposition, I was able to value it more. What I had once thought of as lethargic, I now thought of as calm and relaxed. My respect for Jordan and his temperament grew.

I Won't Let Go

We stopped along the road to see the sunset.

"Wow, that's beautiful!" Margie said breathlessly.

"Yeah, it's really nice."

"Look at all those colors and the patterns. Isn't it fantastic?" she said.

"It's pretty."

"How can you be so unresponsive?"

"What do you want me to do, dance?" I was annoyed.

"Why not? You know, almost the only time I see you expressing real enthusiasm and excitement is when you're watching a sporting event. I'd like some of that excitement in response to me and the things we do together."

Letting go at a game was allowable behavior, but letting go in other situations was risky. If someone thought my emotion was inappropriate, they might say, "That's a dumb way to feel."

If my response made me look childish, someone might say, "You're immature."

If my response moved me deeply enough to cry, someone might say, "What a sissy."

If my response made me feel scared enough to need somebody else to help, someone might say, "He's weak."

If my response just wasn't what they wanted, someone might say, "You're not good enough."

I didn't like being judged. It was safer to keep my responses controlled at a low level than to react spontaneously and risk criticism.

My Strong Exterior Is A Facade

All my life I believed that it was wrong to let other people know when I was anxious, hurt, or scared. It was too risky because it made me too vulnerable. Besides, I believed nobody really wanted to know if I wasn't feeling confident.

It was Jordan's birthday. I planned a surprise dinner at a restaurant with a few of our close friends. After dinner we came back to our house. I had planned the party carefully, but somehow it just wasn't going well. The conversation was strained. The guests seemed restless, as if they were waiting for something to happen—or to find an excuse to go home.

Since it was my party, and therefore my responsibility to make it a success, I was feeling very uptight but I just pretended I was at ease and having fun. I was so involved with masking my feelings and trying to make the party work that I completely forgot about Jordan.

When the last guests left, Jordan exploded with anger. "How could you treat me like that? You just ignored me, and I felt left out at my own party!"

"I was just trying to be a good hostess," I explained. But that only made him angrier, as I seemed more concerned with our guests' feelings than with his.

After much arguing I finally said, "I was tense and nervous." He looked at me in amazement.

"I'm almost always anxious in social situations," I said. "I'm afraid that I won't know what to say. It's especially difficult when it's my party."

"But you're always so relaxed and seem to be having such a good time," he answered.

"It's just a cover-up."

When Jordan was let in on the reason for my behavior his anger dissipated. He asked if there was anything he could do to help me feel more comfortable. I told him that all I needed was for him to put his arm around me and ask if I was feeling okay.

The next time we were out socially and I was nervous, I showed it. Jordan put his arm around me. He didn't try to talk me out of what I felt. His acceptance of my anxiety, without criticism, helped me to become more accepting of myself.

He Feels Good And We Are Well

It had been only a few months since Jordan had started back to school. I couldn't believe the difference in him. By the end of the year he had breezed through graduate school with high praise from his professors and students. A top high school offered him a good teaching position and, within one year, he was honored as the "most popular" teacher.

As Jordan's self-confidence grew, my excited feelings about him grew as well. All of the wonderful, close and loving feelings we'd had when we were first living together were back.

Sex
and
Affection

Getting That Orgasm

In the first few years of our marriage, getting that orgasm was my primary objective whenever we made love. I would approach each sexual encounter wondering whether or not I would have "It" this time.

In order to get It, I would concentrate very hard on my feelings and also on a sexual fantasy. As I got closer to orgasm, sometimes I would say to myself, "I think I'm going to have It now." Bam! Just that thought would be enough to pull me out of my sexual feelings, and I'd be back down to feeling nothing. It was very frustrating.

Jordan was also trying very hard. As I had not yet learned to have an orgasm during intercourse, he brought me to climax either manually or orally. We had to do everything just right. Any noise, sudden move or change in rhythm would back me right down again. To reach an orgasm might take as long as forty-five minutes, and I would become concerned that he was tired or bored. My concern kept me from paying attention to my sexual feelings. By the time I reached an orgasm, both Jordan and I were exhausted. It was work. Hard work for both of us. And it wasn't much fun.

We Begin To Enjoy Sex

We'd been "working" at sex for a few years, and Margie was still taking forever to have an orgasm. Finally I said to her, "Look, all this work is ridiculous. Can't we just relax and enjoy ourselves, and forget about your orgasm? If it happens, it happens, and if it doesn't, it doesn't. Let's just not worry about it for a while, anyway."

Those words must have been magic for her. As soon as she stopped worrying about "succeeding," she started having fun. Our sex became more relaxed, and Margie's orgasms started happening faster and faster. In fact, after a while I said to her, "Hey, slow down! What's your hurry? Let's relax and enjoy each other longer!"

Because Margie took partial responsibility for her difficulty with orgasm right from the beginning, I never felt defensive or inadequate. Had I believed that she held me responsible for her satisfaction, I could never have been as accepting and patient as I was.

\

It's Hard To Ask For Loving

"I'm going upstairs now."

"Okay."

I take a shower, get into bed and wait for Margie. She stays downstairs puttering around and reading.

An hour goes by. I'm becoming more and more upset.

She finally comes upstairs.

I watch her as she gets ready for bed. Finally I explode, "I've been waiting for you for an hour."

"What for?"

"So that we could make love."

"I didn't know you wanted to make love. You didn't say anything to me about it."

"It seems to me there are lots of things you do that are more important than just being with me."

"That's not true. I came upstairs because I wanted to be with you."

"Well then, why didn't you come up earlier?"

"I didn't even know that you wanted me to."

"I told you I was going upstairs."

"That doesn't say anything to me about what you want or expect. You have an expectation that I don't know anything about, and when I don't fulfill it, you get angry and blame me. I don't want to talk about it anymore. I'm going to take a shower."

She had kept me waiting, and I was angry. I hadn't told her what I wanted, and she was angry. Lying in bed with the lights off, I still couldn't sleep.

When Margie finally came to bed, I told her, "You know, it's really hard for me to make an open statement that I want to have sex with you. I say things like, 'How are you feeling tonight?' or 'Are you tired?' or 'What do you feel like doing?' instead of saying, 'I'd like to make love.'"

"Why not just level with me?"

"I guess I'm afraid you're going to say you don't want to. I really feel rejected when you don't want to make love with me, so I try to find out what you're feeling first."

"Okay, I can understand that, but lots of times I don't get the subtle little message. We end up with misunderstandings and arguments rather than lovemaking."

"Okay. Let's make love."

"Not now, I've got a headache . . . I'm kidding, I'm kidding."

Telling Him Just What I Want

Oh dear, intercourse just isn't making it for me tonight. It really isn't feeling too good. Maybe I'm tired. Maybe I'm tense. I wish Jordan would go down on me. Then maybe I'd relax and get into it more. How can I get him to do it? Maybe if I kind of move my body around he'll get the idea. Shit, this is ridiculous. Why don't I just tell him what I want? I wonder why it's so easy to talk to him about my sexual problems, but so hard to be direct about what I want him to do to me?

For a long time I battled inside my head over trying to get Jordan to do what I wanted sexually and maneuvering him into doing it rather than asking him directly.

Jordan finally brought it up. "I wish you would tell me more often what you want me to do to you when we're making love. It excites me when you do."

"But I don't want you to do something just because I ask you to. I want you to do it on your own because you want to do it."

I also couldn't tell Jordan what I wanted for fear he wouldn't want to do it and would be angry that I'd asked. He knew the textbook facts about sex pretty well. But I hadn't let him in on a lot of facts about the way I am sexually. I was afraid if I told him, he wouldn't approve of me and value me for being the way I am.

Jordan told me that he shared the same fears. We had boxed ourselves in, hoping that somehow each of us would guess what the other wanted without our having to say anything. But we weren't mind readers.

When Jordan understood my fears he said, "I promise you that I won't do what you ask unless I really want to."

"You mean you'll tell me if you don't want to?"

"Yes."

"But that's scary too. Maybe I'll feel hurt if you don't want to do something to me that I want."

"We'll have to talk about it, then."

"Okay, but I want you to tell me what you want, too. It makes me feel good to do something to you or for you that you really enjoy."

I Don't Have To Worry About His Erection

Since sex was rather difficult for me in the first few years of our marriage, much of the time I didn't look forward to it. If I was affectionate, I was afraid Jordan would get an erection. I believed that once a man had an erection, he had to have an orgasm. If I refused relief, I felt very guilty, believing that his hard-on and his pain were all my fault.

Sometimes when Jordan would move next to me in bed, I wouldn't respond. When I'd feel his hard penis on my leg or stomach, I'd lie very still, pretending I didn't know it was there, hoping it would go away without causing him too much pain.

Once in a while when I wanted some affection, but not necessarily sex, I'd snuggle up to Jordan in bed or on the couch, and he'd get an erection. Then I'd feel I had to do something about it, and we'd wind up making love.

Much of the time I would shy away from being affectionate except in public, where it was safe.

"You're hardly ever affectionate with me when we're alone," Jordan complained.

"Maybe I'd be more affectionate if we didn't have to have sex every time you get turned on."

"But we don't have to have sex every time I get turned on."

"Won't that be painful for you?"

"Well, if it happened day after day with no release at all, eventually I'd feel some pain, but as long as we have fairly regular sex, it's no problem."

Knowing I don't have to do anything about Jordan's erection has freed me to be as affectionate as I like.

I Need Affection More Than Sex

I had been away from Margie for the weekend.

As I was driving home, I felt very sexual. I fantasized returning home, telling Margie of my sexual desire, and the two of us making love. The rational part of me kept saying, "This can't happen, it's the middle of the afternoon, and she'll have a hundred things to do."

By the time I arrived home I was so consumed by my sexual feelings that I just rushed in and blurted them out to Margie. To my complete surprise she said, "I'd love to."

Almost as soon as I entered her I realized I hadn't wanted sex after all. As we both started to relax, be affectionate and talk of our anxieties about being separated and our excitement at being together again, and as I heard Margie reaffirm her loving feelings for me and tell me how much I was missed, I felt reassured. My sexual feelings diminished. I was content to hold, to touch, to look and to kiss.

I began to think about the confusion between my sexual needs and my needs for affection, comfort and reassurance.

I'd been taught that I should pursue sex, but that affection—simply hugging and touching—wasn't something a man needed. But I do need it, even more than sex.

If I give and receive affection only when I want sex, then much of my need for affection goes unfulfilled.

My Penis Never Lies

We were making love and I lost my erection. I frantically tried to get it back—without success.

"What's the matter?" Margie asked.

"I don't know. I really want to make love."

"Something must be going on or you'd be able to," she said.

"I don't know what's the matter."

"Are you sure?"

"Well, maybe it's the argument we had this morning. I thought I could forget it, but I guess it's still bothering me."

We discussed the issues of the argument until I finally felt that Margie really understood my position. That felt good. We hugged. My body started to relax, and my penis became erect. We became reinvolved in our lovemaking.

For most of my life the desire to have intercourse was so great that other concerns never got in the way. But as my emotions have become more important to me, I've noticed a direct connection between my feelings and my sexuality. My desire to make love is no longer separate from how I'm feeling about myself or about Margie. Any time I lose my erection there is a good reason for it. I can sometimes cover up my feelings, but my penis never lies.

Sex Becomes Boring

"Sex has been kind of boring lately," I hesitantly said to Jordan.

We had talked about an evening of lovemaking, but by the time we got around to it, I was "too tired."

"I've been feeling the same way," Jordan said. "I thought yesterday making love outside in the sun would make it more exciting but it didn't. Something sure as hell is missing."

"You know," he said a moment later, "I think our whole relationship has been boring and routine the last month or so. We haven't been spending much time together, sharing ourselves, talking or having fun—or even arguing."

"Hmm—every time sex is boring, I start thinking that we need to try a new technique. But in the end it always comes down to what's happening between us."

As we talked on we realized that "I'm too tired" and "I'm not feeling well" are often excuses for not wanting to make love, or for not doing something else we may not want to do. Being tired is a great no-conflict excuse. To say "I don't want to" might make trouble, but who can argue with "I'm not feeling well"?

It works the other way too. When our relationship is stimulating and intense, so is our sex. We can do everything in the world to each other physically, but it's not exciting unless we're emotionally involved. Then sex becomes a real and positive expression of how we feel about each other and definitely not boring.

Do You Masturbate?

We were lying in bed talking about a book on sex we'd just read. "Have you masturbated since we've been married?" Jordan asked.

I hesitated before I answered. Would he be hurt if I told him the truth? Would he be angry?

"Yes, once in a while," I said. "Don't you?"

He hesitated too. "Occasionally."

"How come you never told me?"

"I don't know. I guess it just never came up before. I think I've been afraid to say anything—afraid you'd be disappointed in me and yourself."

"I thought you'd feel the same way," I said.

"You know, it's a relief to talk about it," Jordan said. "I do feel guilty when I do it, but there are times when I feel horny or I'm fantasizing and I just want an orgasm without a whole involvement. Do you really feel okay about it?"

"Yes. I've felt guilty too. I assumed that you masturbated because I know that men usually do, but I didn't know how you'd feel about my doing it. I thought you might feel inadequate or insulted if you found out, that you'd think I was doing it because something was wrong with our sex. But there are times when I just want to be alone with my sexuality, when I want to be totally absorbed in it without thinking about you. Sometimes I just want to do it because it feels good and it's different from when we make love. It's certainly not a substitute for it."

"It doesn't seem to have gotten in the way of our lovemaking," Jordan said.

"For sure! Hey! It's not so difficult to talk about, is it?"

Planning Time For Sex

Another full day and evening ended, we flopped exhausted into bed. For weeks we hadn't had any time to ourselves to just relax and make love.

Suddenly the idea of another 11:30 quickie just got to me. "All this clutter of chores and hobbies and other people. It's my fault as much as yours," I told Margie, "but we let all these things crowd out our time for ourselves. Why don't we make love early in the evening, and then we could spend as much time as we want with each other? If we have other things to do, we could do them later in the evening."

"Those other things will never get done," Margie said.

"So what. Those other things are getting in the way of our relationship. Maybe we ought to set aside a time to be together and make love."

"You mean marking it on the calendar like a dinner date? That sounds weird." Margie was skeptical.

"Well, we make time for other things that are a lot less important. Why not lovemaking?"

Just getting used to the idea was difficult. We believed that sexual encounters should be spontaneous. But when sex had to be fitted in with everything else, it was either too hurried or else infrequent.

When we were dating, many of our sexual experiences were planned. We knew that sometime during our time together we would make love. We never discussed it, but we thought about it and it was very stimulating. After a few hours of fun and intimacy, we felt very loving in bed.

We decided to set aside one evening during the week and one evening on the weekend for just the two of us. It was to be unstructured time for us to be involved with each other. Sometime during this two- or three-hour period we would probably make love.

We have come to love our love dates together. Sometimes we go into our bedroom, take off our clothes, and just relax together, holding each other and talking. Other times we play in the shower, bath or jacuzzi. We may just take a walk. As much of this time as we can, we spend together nude. Our time together creates the intimacy necessary for a special sexual experience.

I Want More

After a number of years, intercourse began to feel really good. I enjoyed our lovemaking, but frequently intercourse didn't last long enough for me to reach an orgasm. We had just read about Masters and Johnson's squeeze technique for delaying ejaculation, but I was still concerned about approaching Jordan. The other things had been my problem or our problem, but this somehow was different. He might feel inadequate and become defensive, or perhaps he wouldn't be willing to try and resolve the situation for fear of failing.

I thought about it for months before I got up enough nerve to approach him. I was waiting for the right circumstances. Finally, one night when our sex had been particularly good, I timidly opened up the subject.

"I really love the way we make love, but I want more from it. I'd enjoy having intercourse for a longer time."

Uh oh. He looks like he's been hit over the head with a baseball bat. I guess some things will always be hard to talk about.

I Don't Know If I Can Do It

I had been asking Margie to be more aggressive. "Tell me what you want from our sexual experiences," I would say. Then she told me.

"I'd really enjoy having intercourse for a longer time."

Her request dropped like a bomb. Maybe I should have been satisfied with her the way she was. I felt scared, shocked and disappointed. I thought our sex life had gotten pretty good. It had for me, anyway.

I felt her request was a demand, and it scared the hell out of me. I didn't feel that I could meet her need.

I told her my fears. She assured me she wasn't making a demand. "It's just something I'd like to work toward," she said.

We discussed the squeeze technique. I was still frightened and pessimistic when I agreed to try it, and I wasn't convinced that even if it were successful, there would be much in it for me.

Within a week it started to work.

Making Love

As intercourse lasted longer, a whole new dimension to our lovemaking opened up.

During these experiences there are no goals; there is no rush to orgasm. We are able to pleasure each other's bodies while having intercourse, finding different ways to touch, new places to explore. Because we can take the time, the variety of experiences available to us has increased immeasurably.

When we create warm and loving feelings between us before and during our lovemaking, we find it easier to relax, to smile, to have fun, to tell each other what we want and to express our feelings.

At those times when we fully combine our emotions with our physical senses, our lovemaking builds in its intensity and passion and we become acutely aware of the sensuality of each other's bodies. We are free to reach spontaneously to each other, and lovemaking becomes truly making love.

Pregnancy and Children

I'm Not Ready For A Baby

"I think I'm pregnant."

"How did that happen? I mean I know how it happened, but we've been so careful. What happened?"

"Well, I'm not sure, but I checked my diaphragm and there's a tiny hole in it. That's all it takes."

"How do you feel about it?"

"I'm delighted. And it's only three months earlier than we'd planned."

"Yeah, but now you have to quit teaching before the end of the semester, and we can't afford that."

"We'll manage somehow. Don't worry."

Don't worry, she says. Even with our combined teaching salaries we're barely making it financially. We just took on the tremendous expense of our own home, we've got no money in the bank, we're going to have a baby, we're going to lose three months of her salary, I don't know if I'll be able to find a job for the summer, and she says not to worry.

For me, a baby meant more responsibilities and more restrictions. I was scared and depressed and angry with Margie, but I couldn't tell her. It wasn't really her fault. It was wrong to be angry with her, but I was, and I withdrew.

He Doesn't Care About The Baby

I had always wanted a baby. I had had two miscarriages in my first marriage, which left me with the enormous fear that I would never bear children. When I became pregnant I was terribly excited, but frightened that I would miscarry again. I needed a lot of comfort and reassurance from Jordan. I didn't get it.

When he came home from work, Jordan would spend hours with our dog Moose, playing with him and showering him with affection. I was jealous. Moose was getting what I wanted. If I told Jordan explicitly what I wanted, he might have given it to me out of obligation rather than out of genuine enthusiasm. I didn't feel I really had a right to expect more from him. I had always represented myself as a strong person, and I felt I should be able to handle this by myself. At the time I didn't realize how desperately I wanted Jordan to want the baby and how important his involvement and excitement were to me. I was vaguely aware of my sadness, but I never shared it with him. I decided to handle things by myself.

Despite Jordan's lack of concern, after the first three months—when my tiredness and fears of miscarriage had abated—I was relaxed and contented. I loved looking at my belly in the mirror. I was ecstatic when I felt the baby move within me, and I tried to pull Jordan into my excitement. "Hey! Feel the baby! He sure can kick!" He remained uninterested.

I took classes and read books about raising children. Jordan was interested in the books but not in me. I immersed myself in my teaching and my pregnancy, and our relationship lapsed into a dull routine. As the time for delivery approached, my only fear was that Jordan would remain uninvolved after the birth. I could handle the pregnancy alone, but I knew I desperately needed him to be involved with the child.

The Joy Of Fatherhood

During Margie's pregnancy I worried about whether I would ever care about our child-to-be.

But when Eric was three weeks old he smiled at me. He became a reality with that smile, and I was captivated. Moose wasn't nearly as interesting as this fascinating and lovable little person. I hurried home each day to play with my baby and wait for his smile. When he cried I wanted to give him to his mother, but I learned, reluctantly, to change and bathe him. Margie and I had so much to share and talk about.

As if by magic, all of my intensity and enthusiasm had come flooding back for Eric and for his wonderful mother.

The Shock Of Motherhood

Nothing had prepared me for the shock of motherhood.

Before Eric was born, I had been an art teacher, and before that I had spent exciting years at college. Life had always offered lots of opportunities and stimulation.

Free time had always been important—and available. There were lots of things I wanted to do, both alone and with Jordan, and they all took time—a lot of time. I never counted how much.

Then Eric was born, and I had no more time.

I had read lots of books on breast-feeding and child-raising, and I felt I had it all down pat. I thought I knew just what it would be like, but those books never told me how many hours a baby consumed. They made it sound so simple and gratifying. They never talked about baby-sitting problems, or how difficult a hungry baby can be in a market, or how little some of them sleep. They never told me how much this demanding baby would change my relationship with my husband, how he would rob me of time alone and us of time together. They never told me that I would almost always be tired.

Suddenly we had a whole new set of problems that weren't in the index of Dr. Spock or any other book I'd read.

I loved Eric dearly, and all the universal joys were there. But while I was finding all these new joys, my own need to create and accomplish was going unmet, and I was very unhappy.

Out Of The Doldrums

To begin to understand and change my situation took six months of long discussions with Jordan.

I finally hired a cleaning woman once a week and was able to take a painting class and a psychology class on the day she was there. My mother came twice a week to take care of Eric while I substitute-taught to earn the money to pay for the cleaning woman, my classes, and other daytime babysitting.

I decided to earn more money by having a Christmas ceramic sale. Between Jordan, my mother, and various sitters, I found the time to make enough for a huge sale. It was so much more successful than I had anticipated that Jordan, eighteen-month-old Eric and I were able to spend ten days in Hawaii.

My doldrums were over, for a while. And I felt we could plan for another child.

How Could He Do That To Me?

Almost two years after Eric was born, I became pregnant again. I fully expected Jordan to be as completely involved and excited as I was. After all, he had experienced the joys of fatherhood and now knew what to expect. Again I had become pregnant before we had planned, and again Jordan withdrew.

This time I was even more hurt, disappointed, and confused.

Once more, neither of us confronted the issue during the pregnancy.

Toward the end as we took prepared childbirth classes together, Jordan became more involved and the actual birth was very exciting for both of us.

It was through these classes that I began to believe that it was all right to want Jordan's concern. And it was his participation in these classes and in Joshua's birth that allowed Jordan to finally open up. But it took a long time.

A year later we were away together for the weekend, talking about having a third child. Suddenly I was aware of the full force of what had happened during the pregnancies, and I began to cry bitterly. I cried for a long time, pouring out to him all my resentment and hurt at his apparent lack of caring.

Finally, Jordan told me how much he had resented my getting pregnant before we had planned, and that he now realized that he had been punishing me with his lack of involvement.

"I feel terrible now that I see how I've hurt you. I'd really like to go through another pregnancy and this time be involved in it."

As we talked, I revealed another important thing to Jordan that I had never told him.

"As I became more and more pregnant, especially the second time, I felt terribly sexual. In the last few months I wanted a release every day. I didn't sleep well unless I'd had an orgasm and since you were so uninvolved with me, I masturbated almost daily. I was afraid that if I told you how sexual I was feeling, you wouldn't want to make love that often. So I never told you."

"I feel awful realizing how much in our relationship I missed. You know I love it when you're sexual, but when I'm withdrawn I'm not very interested in sex."

We held each other and cried together. We had both allowed this to happen for our own reasons. We would not let it happen again.

We Did It!

When Margie burst into my classroom and excitedly threw her arms around me, I knew we were going to have a little girl. We'd waited five agonizing weeks for that phone call telling us what our unborn child would be.

"It's a girl," I announced to my class. "You can all go home now." Margie and I embraced warmly, half crying with the knowledge that our hard work and persistence had paid off.

After our two sons, we both very much wanted a girl. Since I had already fathered three sons, the first from my former marriage, the chance of our having a girl seemed less than 50-50. Babies for adoption were scarce, and to specify the sex of the child made the wait unreasonable.

Then we learned about the theory that a child's sex was determined by the relationship of intercourse to ovulation, and we decided to go ahead and try it.

First Margie needed to learn to predict her ovulation time, and it took six months of persistent temperature charting to do it. Finally, on the right day, we tried for the baby we so much wanted.

We conceived on our first try, and then the waiting began.

The results of an amniocentesis done in Margie's fourteenth week of pregnancy identified the sex of our Sheryl. We celebrated her before she arrived. We are still celebrating.

The Gift That Keeps On Giving

"We want more time with you," our children complained to us.

It was Sunday and we had been home all day, playing with them, reading to them, talking with them. At 8:30 they still wanted to play with us, but Jordan and I had planned to spend the evening alone together.

"No," Jordan answered. "Now I want to be alone with Mommy. It's important for us to have time alone together. We spent a lot of time with you today, and now we want time for each other."

They were angry and didn't want to go to bed.

"Fine," I said. "You don't have to go to bed, but we're going into our room and we want to be alone."

A few minutes later they called and wanted to be kissed goodnight.

It is vital for the children to know that Jordan's and my relationship is important, that it is the backbone of our family.

The best parenting we can give our children is for them to see that we have a relationship with each other that's loving. If we always put aside our own needs in order to meet theirs, we would probably end up with nothing between us, with no involvement for them to see.

As much as the children may not like the time we spend together away from them, we believe it makes it more comfortable for them to be in this family. They know that they are not responsible for Jordan or me. We are not their burden. They know our happiness is not entirely dependent on them, but on each other. They can grow up and leave us with the knowledge that for us, our relationship is the abiding one—the one that remains even when they leave.

This does not mean that we always put our needs before our children's. Often, especially when they were very young, we put aside our own needs in order to meet theirs. But now we set aside time for our involvement with them in addition to the time we need for ourselves.

When we are with our children, it is because we want to be. We tend to them out of love, not obligation. They will never be made to feel guilty for their existence. We will never say to them, "Look at all we've given you, how come you don't appreciate it?" or "If it hadn't been for you, we could have . . . ."

Time Alone

"Who wants time alone with me tonight?"

"I do," yells Sheryl.

"No, me," says Josh.

"I want time alone with Mommy," says Eric.

Sheryl and Josh and I go into Josh's room to read books, play games, and talk about our day. Eric and Margie go outside to play catch.

Time alone when the children have our full attention has become very important in our house. We try not to answer the phone or even to think about other things. Rather, we try to focus our attention fully on the children, to be open and totally available to them alone.

It's so easy, with our busy lives, to end up not spending much quality time with our children, and when this happens, they become far more difficult to handle. In an effort to get attention we have not freely given, they will fight more, complain more, and demand more of us. But when we spend concentrated time with them, it seems easier for them to amuse themselves. When they know they will have their hour of Time Alone, we hear less often the request "Play with me, play with me."

Because they've come to understand how important it is to them to have time alone with us, they've also come to understand and respect the fact that we need time alone with each other. When we say, "Mommy and I need time alone together," they are far more likely to respect our needs when their needs for time with us have been met.

Our Children See Us Nude

"Don't let your children see you nude," said the nursery school director. "It's too sexually arousing for them, especially after the age of five. They just can't handle it."

"Maybe she's right," I thought, so I started putting on a robe as soon as I got out of bed in the morning. For some reason this just didn't feel natural for me.

"How do you feel about our children seeing us nude?" I asked Jordan.

"I want them to. I never saw my parents nude. I felt the body was to be hidden, and to see it and enjoy it was taboo. I hope our children will know that their bodies are not something to be ashamed of. How are they going to feel that if we hide ours?"

"But what about our nudity being sexually arousing?"

"Well," Jordan said, "I just don't think that's true. Perhaps if parents are provocative, the child may be aroused, but nudity in itself isn't sexual. Let's see what happens."

Our children don't seem to notice whether or not we're nude. If we're getting out of bed, sunbathing, or swimming, they expect it. The problem was ours, not theirs.

Mommy And Daddy Are Going To Make Love Now

"Mommy and Daddy are going to make love now. Please don't disturb us."

Margie and I decided that it was important for our children to know that we make love, and that it is something we both look forward to and enjoy. We spent many hours discussing this concept before we actually put it into practice.

"I could never imagine my parents making love," Margie said. "I don't remember hearing them talk about it. They were so secretive. I would have liked to know if it was a joyful part of their marriage, especially for my mother. It certainly would have helped me form a more positive sexual self-concept. But since they never talked about their own sexuality, it was hard to ask questions."

"I know," I said. "That's why I want our children to know about all the aspects of our relationship. They hear us argue, so why shouldn't they also know we make love?"

"Do you think they might be harmed in any way if they knew?"

"I can't think of any reason not to tell them. It seems they might be harmed by not seeing lovemaking as a positive, important part of a relationship. So I'm for being open with them about what we do and how we feel about it."

When Eric was about four years old, we read him a book about how babies are made. After finishing the book we told him, "People don't make love just when they want to have a baby. Mommy and I make love a lot because we love each other and because it feels good. Making love is a very special thing that we do with each other. If you come to our room and the door is locked, we are probably making love. We like to be alone when we do that."

Each child has heard essentially the same thing.

Our children seem to understand and accept the fact that we make love and enjoy it. So when we say, "We're going to make love now," they nod and usually leave us alone.

We used to make love wondering when they would come bursting in on us with an emergency. We finally realized that as much as we didn't like locks on doors, we needed one on ours. They know that if there is an emergency they can disturb us, but that our time alone together is very important to us.

When we tell our children that we need time alone together, they are often willing to take care of each other. One Sunday morning, Joshua, then four and a half, walked into our bedroom while we were cuddling. We said, "Josh, we'd like some more time alone."

"Oh," he said matter-of-factly, as he walked out and shut the door, "you're going to make love." Josh and Eric took care of Sheryl while we had our time alone.

Occasionally, as the family sits around the dinner table talking about the day, we may mention how much we enjoyed our time together, especially when we made love. Our children are not shocked. They are informed and aware. They are growing up knowing that we make love and enjoy it as a natural part of our marriage.

Responsibility and Equality

A Not-So-Innocent Question

We were getting ready to go on a picnic. Getting
ready meant that I would get myself ready and that
Margie would get herself ready and our children ready
and prepare and pack whatever we were taking with us.
On this particular day, I decided to make what I thought
was a very generous offer.

"What can I do to help you?" I asked.

She blew up at me, "I don't want you to help me!"

"That's a hell of a way to say thanks," I snapped
back.

"Thanks for what? For not knowing what has to be
done?" she countered.

After the battle ended, and we were sifting through
the ashes, Margie explained, "When you asked to help, I
felt like a parent doling out chores. I need you to take
enough interest in the activities of our house to know
what needs to be done and to do it, whether it's preparing
for a picnic, changing the baby's diaper, arranging for our
sons to have friends over, or whatever else is going on. I
need you to take some responsibility for things around
here."

I had never thought about my responsibilities in
those terms before, but I could see that she was right. My
images of what I should be controlled so much of my
behavior. Traditional definitions of the duties of a man,
husband, father determined what I felt comfortable
doing. Margie, too, operated within the "normal" bounds
of woman, mother, wife. Although neither of us liked the
socially imposed cubbyholes, we had accepted them
without questioning. Now we wanted to do something
about it. We talked about the major areas of our lives,
who had responsibility for which area, and our feelings
about it.

I had accepted the total responsibility for starting our lovemaking and arousing Margie sexually. I hated that role, and initiating sex had become a chore.

Margie took the total responsibility for the house, but she hated it. The needs of a house never seemed to end, and so she rarely relaxed and enjoyed being at home.

I had fallen heir to total responsibility for planning how we spent our time. It irritated me that Margie rarely thought of things for us to do together.

Margie had total responsibility for arranging the children's schedules—carpools for school, social engagements—and tending to literally all of their practical needs. The endless details took a lot of her time.

I had the total responsibility for earning the money for our family, and I felt boxed in. I wanted the freedom to change jobs or work less if I wanted to without causing the family a great deal of hardship.

We wanted each other to actively participate and share as equally as possible in the major areas of our lives. And we began to make the effort.

I Tried It And I Didn't Like It

"Why don't you try it for one day and then let's talk."

Margie was angry. We were arguing about how we spent our time during the day. I went to school every morning and taught a full day. She had nothing to do except take care of our house and two children. I could never understand what was so difficult about her life. In fact, it made me angry when she complained, because I actually envied her. And I told her so.

"You don't have to get up and go out to work every day," I said. "Your time isn't structured. You can relax when you want to, and you've got the comforts of home all around you. It all seems ideal to me."

"You just try it and see how ideal it is," she said.

"All right, I will," I replied, not too concerned about being called on to fulfill the bargain.

Margie seized the opportunity to test me when we heard about an all-day Saturday/Sunday workshop that both of us wanted to attend. I was the one who usually went to such workshops, but this time she would go.

Saturday morning, Eric, who was four and a half, Josh, who was two, and I happily waved goodbye to Mommy. It was a pleasant day, relatively calm and uneventful although I was vaguely frustrated. Every time I tried to get to the book I was reading for class or to just relax, one of the children needed something, it was time for a meal, or there was a dispute to resolve.

By the time I made dinner, gave the boys their baths, helped them on with their pajamas and tucked them in bed, it was eight o'clock. After cleaning up the kitchen and straightening the house, I took a shower, settled into bed with my book, and waited for Margie. With all of its small annoyances, the day hadn't seemed that bad. I still couldn't understand what she had to complain about.

At 10:05 Margie burst into the bedroom, high from the excitement of her day and eager to share it with me.

She went on and on about what had happened, whom she had met, and what they had talked about. I tried to share her enthusiasm, but I really wanted to tell her about my day. Finally she ran down and asked me how my day had been. "Well," I said, "Eric and Josh had a fight but they ate nicely, and Joshua had two BM's and . . ." I found myself hating her.

She'd had a great day that left her flushed with excitement. Mine was nothing compared to that. Suddenly I understood what she'd been missing. She'd had a steady diet of baby talk, and she needed the time and freedom to talk with interesting adults. She needed opportunities for intellectual stimulation and growth. And, for a day, she had had them.

Sunday I saw her off with mixed feelings. I was glad she would have another day of challenge and stimulation but I resented being housebound again. I was getting an understanding of Margie's life that could only come from experience, but I would be glad to get back to my own world on Monday.

I Hate Being Told What To Do

Monday: "Hon, will you fix the toilet, please?"
"Yeah. Okay."

Wednesday: "Have you fixed the toilet yet?"
"I haven't had a chance."

Saturday: "How about that damn toilet?"
"Later."

Sunday: A fight because it hasn't been fixed yet.

I hate being told what to do. I don't say, "No, I won't do that." To avoid conflict, I agree. Then I just don't do it.

Margie says she hates to beg me to do the chores that need doing. "I always wind up feeling like a mother to you."

"When you ask me or tell me what to do, I resent you. It's like a power struggle, and if I do what you want then you win and I lose," I said.

We understood each other's feelings, but that didn't get things done. We needed to come up with a way to avoid this kind of conflict. We agreed to have Margie make a list of the things she wanted me to do. Unless I objected to the task then and there, I would get it done.

Margie agreed not to ask me about the chore once it was on the list, and not to criticize the job that I did. The list was posted with a magnet on our refrigerator door. When I finished the job, I would cross it off the list. We would have no verbal communication about it.

For years we used the list successfully. Without direct verbal communication I had no need to rebel.

Eventually Margie could ask me directly to do something, and I could respond without resentment.

But don't ask me to fix your toilet.

Nice Girls Can Be Sexual

"How come you hardly ever initiate our sexual experiences?" Jordan asked.

"I don't know," I answered.

Even though I was enjoying sex, I still didn't initiate it very often.

The messages I'd received as a child from home, school, TV, movies, and friends were clear: "Don't be sexual until you're married. Keep a lid on your sexual feelings. You're a bad girl if you feel sexual and even worse if you act on your sexual impulses." The messages worked—the lid clamped tightly shut.

When I got married the lid did not just unclamp itself and fall away. I had to pry it off. After all those years of saying "No" to myself sexually, it was very hard to say "Yes."

Initiating sex is the exact opposite of what I'd been taught. It's like saying, "I'm sexual and I'm willing to show you how sexual. I'm willing to do things to turn you on. I'm willing to take responsibility for being sexual rather than just letting it happen to me."

Now when I allow myself to be sexually aggressive, I'm more sexual than at any other time, because I've taken the responsibility.

Now . . . where's Jordan?

She'll Drive Us To The Poorhouse

"We need a new stereo," Margie said.

"That's ridiculous! You want to spend five hundred dollars for a new stereo, and you don't even listen to our old one."

"But all our friends are putting in beautiful sound systems."

"Look, you know we can't afford to spend five hundred dollars. Why do you bring it up?"

"You are so tight I can't believe it. You don't want to spend money on anything."

Another argument about money.

For the first five years of our marriage we had very few hassles about money. In fact, one of the things that appealed to me most about Margie was her seeming lack of interest in possessions. When she told me she could be happy living on a teacher's salary, I was convinced. We had settled comfortably into a modest lifestyle. Now it seemed like every week she wanted us to buy something new. I was outraged—we not only couldn't afford these things, we didn't need them.

I had seen women all around me—relatives and friends—pushing their husbands to make more and more money to pay for luxuries their husbands didn't want. One of my worst fears was coming true.

One Thing Money Can't Buy

For six months we argued and stewed about money. I realized there was a certain amount of truth in what Jordan was saying—we didn't really need all the things I wanted—but still, I wanted them. They had become very important to me.

Then one evening during a camping trip to Ensenada, as we were lying in our camper having still another argument about money, the discussion shifted to a seemingly unrelated area.

"I resent the fact that you've been spending so much time away from home," I told Jordan.

Jordan had become deeply involved in a very successful drug rehabilitation program he had created for teenagers. His nights and weekends were filled with people to help, talks to be given, fund-raising events, and all the details of running an organization.

With the teenagers Jordan was intense and alive. His intensity was the thing I loved most about him, but I wasn't getting much of it. Our once close relationship was slowly becoming routine and distant. I realized that I had begun to fill up my life with other things, like material objects, which at least gave me momentary pleasure.

That night in the camper we became aware that if we continued in this pattern of separateness, it might well lead to the breakup of our marriage or to a sterile unfulfilling relationship between two strangers.

We worked out a plan that we hoped would meet the needs of both of us. We would start spending two evenings a week alone with each other, and I would become more involved with Jordan's drug program.

This plan was the beginning of our work together developing our approach to therapy.

As we spent more time with each other, my desire for material things subsided.

But our money conflicts were not yet over.

We still had problems about responsibility, and resentment still smoldered over who spent what.

A Working Wife

As I worked more in Jordan's drug rehabilitation program, I realized that it was solving a number of problems for me.

It gave me something rewarding to do besides just take care of our children. It gave me good feelings about myself because I had something unique to offer.

Jordan had recently received his license as a Marriage, Family and Child Counselor, so we decided to start a private practice specializing in sexual problems. We had attended workshops and read everything in the field, and our own difficulties had given us more than an academic acquaintance with the subject. That was tremendously important for the kind of work we planned to do. And we loved working together.

As our practice grew, even more of our problems were being resolved. Jordan was able to give up the total responsibility for earning the money, and cut his teaching to half-time. I was able to give up the total responsibility for the house since we could now afford more household help. Jordan had more time to be with the children, and I had more time for creative projects.

I was happy in our new way of life.

I'll Never Be Able To Afford Her Enthusiasms

Margie came flying home. Throwing her arms around me, she announced ecstatically, "I just saw the most beautiful antique rocking chair and I want you to come with me and see it. It's just what we've been looking for!"

"Well, calm down and tell me about it," I said. My lack of enthusiasm brought her down abruptly. She quietly told me about the chair. I agreed to go see it with her.

As we were driving to the antique store, she exploded with hurt and anger. "Every time I come home feeling really good about something I've bought or that I'm thinking about buying, you never become happy and excited too. When you don't react to me I feel deflated. It takes all the joy out of the experience."

We talked on—to the antique store, through it, and back home again. I finally realized what I'd been worried about. If I were to let myself go and be excited with her, I'd encourage Margie to spend more money. By withholding my enthusiasm, I hoped to hold her in check. I fantasized her being so excited and happy that she would have no regard for our financial situation and just spend money indiscriminately.

I wanted to control our financial future because I feared it would end in chaos if I didn't. Besides, I was still earning most of the money, and therefore I felt I had the right to determine what we should buy and how much we should spend.

Margie didn't agree. Boy, did she not agree!

Sharing The Pursestrings

Time and again, year after year, we'd argue about whether or not I was a frivolous spender.

"I buy hardly any clothes," I'd yell at Jordan. "I never buy furniture without first discussing it with you. I can't understand what you're so uptight about. I'm not the one in this family who wants expensive things. I hate it when I occasionally buy something I really want, and you're so angry about it."

"How do you expect me to budget if you just buy something whenever you want to? I've got to have some control over what you spend!"

By this time we'd been working together a number of years, and I was earning just as much as Jordan. I felt that because he was no longer totally responsible for our income, he shouldn't have total control. Yet he continued to get angry over my occasional unplanned purchases.

Finally after many more conflicts we hit on a solution.

"I want a sum of money each month to do whatever I want with," I told him. "I want to be able to buy something you think is dumb without getting hassled about it. I want to be able to bury it in the backyard if I feel like it."

"Okay. If I know that the amount is limited each month, I can feel comfortable that you're not going to drive us into debt."

We shared the responsibility for earning money, and now we shared the privilege of deciding how to use it.

The Freedom To Goof

"Why do I always have to plan the social schedule? I'd like you to come up with something once in a while." Jordan had said it more than one time.

Finally, one Saturday I suggested we try a new restaurant at the beach that I'd heard about.

Jordan grumbled through a very poor meal, and as we left the restaurant he said, "How did you find that place? You must have really worked at it."

I felt terrible. "Listen," I exploded, "why should I take the responsibility for making plans if you put me down when they turn out badly? Maybe that's why I don't make plans very often."

We decided that if one of us took the responsibility for planning an evening or a vacation or anything and it turned out to be a bummer, we would make the best of it and not criticize the other person.

Since then, although we've each come up with some real duds, we've been able to laugh about the worst of them. Our pact has given us the freedom to suggest many new things without worrying about the consequences of our choice.

Equality Can't Be Given

Jordan and I had been working together for four years, and we needed to ask a favor of one of the doctors who refers clients to us. "You call. He respects you more. You're a man," I said.

"What makes you think he respects me more just because I'm a man?"

"It's just a feeling I have." I've always felt that society—men and women both—values a man's intelligence more than a woman's. I feel I have to prove that what I have to say is as valuable as what a man, almost any man, has to say.

As I grew up, the adults around me seemed to be saying, "We don't expect as much of you as we do of boys. You can grow up and get married and have a family, so it's not important for you to accomplish anything."

I think I do a lot of things in a constant effort to prove my worth, my equality. Often when I sit down with a male client, I feel that he sees me as basically less than himself until I prove to him that I know what I'm talking about. These feelings often affect how I act with men.

God! How I hate those feelings!

I want to say to men, "Value me equally because I'm a woman, not in spite of being a woman."

I want to say to men, "Don't put me in a box and impose a role on me."

I want to say to men, "See past how I look to how I think."

I want to say to men, "Respect my judgment as much as you respect a man's."

I want to say to men, "Don't expect me to be less in order to make you more."

I want to say to men, "Give me my equality," but I realize that it's not possible. As long as they are in a position to give it to me, they are one up.

Equality doesn't come easy. Just because I earn as much as Jordan and he takes care of the children as much as I do, doesn't mean that I feel equal. That is still a struggle. As long as I feel that I have to prove I'm as worthwhile as a man, I don't feel equal.

Equality is not something that can be given. I am equal only when I feel equal.

Control
and
Conflict

That Damn Look

We were at a party given by some of Jordan's students. It had been a long time since we'd been dancing.

"Come on," I said to Jordan, "let's dance!"

"I don't want to."

One of the kids asked me to dance and I accepted. After a few minutes I glanced over at Jordan. He was watching us.

Uh oh—there's that look. He doesn't like what I'm doing. Maybe he thinks my dancing is too sexy. Maybe I shouldn't be dancing like this with teenagers when I'm a married woman. I guess I better stop dancing.

Jordan's look scared the shit out of me.

It was the same look my mother, my grandmother, and my teachers had given me when they disapproved of something I was doing. A kind of angry, withdrawn, pinched-in look. They were able to control my behavior by that look. It meant, "You're a bad girl. You'd better stop what you're doing or I won't like you." All my life I had watched people's faces to see if they approved or disapproved of me. If I got approval one minute, I felt good, but I kept my eye on them just to make sure they were still looking at me the same way.

I was unaware of how I had allowed Jordan's look to control me until two major changes in my life brought our relationship into sharp and painful focus.

Our System

It must have happened very early in our relationship—we're not sure when—a subtle, unspoken agreement on how we would act with each other. Neither of us was consciously aware that we had developed a system, a set way of responding to each other, based around our fears of the consequences of being free and independent.

I feared that if Margie ever acted spontaneously, she might do things that would make me feel terrible.

If I didn't control her, she might then spend too much money; she might behave socially in a way that would embarrass me; she might become intellectually involved with other people and find me less exciting; she might even become emotionally or sexually involved with another man.

If I didn't control her I might be left out or left behind. These fears reflected the self-doubts I had carried around all my life.

Therefore, to protect myself I needed to regulate her behavior.

Sometimes I Don't Know What I Want

Jordan's approval was important to me.

He didn't give it freely.

Only when I behaved in ways that didn't disturb him would he give me his wholehearted loving.

I bought the system to gain his approval.

It was easy to become a willing participant. I, too, was afraid of what I might do were I to function freely. Would I shirk my responsibilities? Would I act foolishly in public? Would I have an affair? Within our system, however, I didn't have to know what I really wanted to do or not do, or whether something was right or wrong, appropriate or inappropriate. It was so easy to let Jordan decide for me.

Jordan decided a lot of things for me. Most of the time, instead of determining for myself what I wanted to buy and what I didn't, I'd say, "Well, I can't buy that because he wouldn't like it." I was, of course, making a decision, but I was refusing to take responsibility for it.

If I knew Jordan would object to my trying a new experience, then I never seriously considered whether it was important to me or not. I just didn't do it. If I did branch out once in a while, his disapproval was so strong that it wasn't worth it.

Had I recognized that we were locked into this system, I would surely have been unhappy about it. But I didn't realize that I let Jordan control so much of my behavior, nor did I realize how I so often was able to control his behavior with my tears or depression.

For eight years we had created a very exclusive marriage to protect ourselves from disturbing experiences, especially relating to other people. We had some disagreements—typical ones over money, sex and children—but for the most part our relationship was peaceful, happy, satisfying. Our marriage was far better than we had ever imagined marriage could be.

As long as we were unaware of our system, it worked well for both of us.

If It's New, It's Dangerous

After eight years and three children, Margie was leaving home.

She had decided to go back to school to earn her master's degree and license in marriage and family counseling, and was very excited.

From the moment school began, however, I saw the profound effects this decision would have on our relationship, and I was immediately apprehensive.

I had things almost exactly as I wanted them, and I needed to be "on guard" to keep the status quo. Each change in our lives, whether it was a new child or a new idea, was a potential enemy that could upset the delicate balance of our system.

Margie was only gone one day a week, but she was now involved with exciting new people and ideas. As a housewife and mother, she had always read a lot, and our work provided her with stimulation and satisfaction, but I was the one with the freedom to meet many interesting people and attend graduate school. Now she was going to step out, and I was worried about the changes it might bring about in our relationship.

I had seen many relationships disturbed or destroyed when one of the partners experienced something new. Friends whose marriages seemed good while the husband was in school started having trouble when he became established in his profession. Marriages disintegrated when one of the partners went into therapy. Wives who went to work or back to school after many years of being home put a strain on the marriage.

I liked our marriage the way it was, so I fought for Margie in the only way I knew. I tried to hold her back.

My Friend

It was my first day of school. I was nervous and excited. I sat down and glanced around the room at the unfamiliar faces.

My eyes stopped. There was Barbara!

Jordan had introduced me to Barbara eight years ago. I knew her only briefly before she married and moved up north. But I had liked her right away. She was an antique dealer then; and she had helped me find some pressedback chairs and make a parquet table top. Now we obviously had even more in common, and as the weeks went by we began to spend a lot of time together. For the first time since I married Jordan, there was another person I really wanted to be with.

Barbara is a very bright and extremely perceptive woman, with an extraordinary sense of humor and ability to have fun. I had never before met another woman with whom I could talk so freely and intensely, or with whom I could laugh with such abandon.

I started spending a couple of mornings a week with her. We'd play tennis and talk, or make the rounds of the antique shops and talk, or work with clay and talk. When I came home, anxious to share my morning with Jordan, he was cold and withdrawn. If I tried to tell him some of the interesting things Barbara and I discussed, he wouldn't respond, acting as if I weren't there.

I hated what was happening between us, but I was not willing to give up my friendship with Barbara.

Her Friend, Not Mine

I hated Margie's relationship with Barbara from the beginning. I didn't like Barbara and I didn't trust her.

I had run into her off and on, through family acquaintances, since I was fifteen years old. There was something captivating but threatening about her. She was exciting and creative, and very humorous, but I was always wary.

Despite my apprehensions, I had entered into a business venture with her when I was twenty-five years old. I wanted to believe that she knew what she was talking about. I invested money, had great dreams for success, and lost everything.

Two years of dreaming and working left me disillusioned and feeling bad about myself for being so gullible. Just when my dreams were being shattered, I met Margie. She met Barbara and then Barbara moved away and that was the last we saw of her. Until now.

Barbara was back in my life and I wanted her out.

Let Sleeping Dogs Lie

Peace at all costs.

For me, an ideal relationship was one where there was no fighting.

I was afraid that once I brought something out into the open, I'd have to deal with it. If it turned out that I couldn't resolve the issue, it might lead to unhappiness and maybe even the destruction of our marriage. I was also afraid if I told Margie what made me unhappy about her, she might tell me, to an even greater extent, what made her unhappy about me. Then I might have to change.

I was also afraid that I wouldn't be able to hold my own in an emotional conflict. To show my emotions, to reveal that I felt hurt, scared, weak, or needing was still unacceptable to my concept of masculinity.

Besides, women always seemed better at expressing feelings. Since I didn't really want to know what I was feeling or needing, it was foolish and dangerous to enter a battle with a competent warrior on her home ground.

Most conflicts seemed to be win-lose situations. Naturally, I wasn't going to start something when there was a good chance that I'd lose. I was prepared to live my entire life never risking a serious conflict.

Peace at all costs.

I Can't Stand An Unresolved Issue

Conflict has always been a frightening experience for me. Often when someone confronts me I get so scared that my body shakes and my teeth chatter. You'd think that because of this I would go out of my way to avoid conflicts. The fact is, once I become aware of it, I've never been able to pretend that a problem doesn't exist.

The first eight years of our marriage were fairly smooth, with relatively few serious conflicts. Those we did have were either calm discussions or mild battles. We always eventually found a way to resolution, and always felt closer and more intimate as a result.

As the years went on I developed two important beliefs which lessened my fears about conflict. The first was that there is no possibility of intimacy without conflict. If we constantly avoid dealing with problem areas, they will increase until we cannot communicate. If we avoid talking about sexual differences, or money problems, or our unhappiness with how we are being treated, our resentment will pile up and our intimacy will have no chance to grow. Without conflict, without open discussion, we would miss one of the most important and productive ways of knowing each other.

The second belief was that there is always a positive way out of a conflict. It need not end in disaster; if Jordan and I kept at it long enough, we would find our way back to good feelings.

Jordan didn't want to confront the problems we were now having, so his withdrawal from conflict itself became a source of conflict between us.

It's Easier To Blame Her

"What's the matter?"

"Nothing."

"You seem distant."

"I'm fine."

We had that exchange many times whenever I was hurt or scared and didn't want to let Margie in on it.

Exposing my hurt or fear was frightening. Margie might be disappointed in me. She might say, "How can you feel that way?" When I thought my response was wrong, I was afraid she would judge me as I judged myself.

Rather than risk being put down, talked out of my feelings, or fighting, I withdrew.

Margie soon perceived this and asked, "What's the matter? You seem distant." When I said "Nothing," I really felt nothing. If she persisted she could usually draw me into a confrontation by being affectionate and sympathetic. If she took the responsibility for the encounter and became open, I felt free to make the accusation I was withholding.

If she accepted my "Nothing" and left me alone, I took this to mean that she didn't care, since she knew that something was wrong. As I became more uncomfortable in my withdrawn state, I began to build a case to justify any angry outburst. I wanted to hurt her and make her feel bad for hurting me.

Whether she chose to leave me alone, or be open and comforting, I had her where I wanted her. I could blame her either way.

It's Easier To Blame Him

Monday: "You seem distant," I said to Jordan.

"No. I'm just tired."

I accept that answer but sense that something else is going on.

Tuesday: "You really do seem distant. Does it have something to do with me?"

"No. Really, nothing's wrong. I just feel hassled about time. There are too many things to do."

Wednesday: "Come on now. I know there's something wrong."

"Well, if there is, I don't know what."

I accept that he doesn't know. Maybe I'm crazy. Maybe I'm perceiving something that doesn't exist.

Thursday: "Listen. You're really withdrawn from me, so it must have something to do with me."

I'm put off again, and again I accept it.

Friday: "You're a shit! You've been withdrawn from me all week, and it's hurting me. I've been asking you for days and you're not willing to deal with it."

I'm frustrated and confused. I cry.

As time went on, I became aware of a whole repertoire of behavior that I had developed in response to Jordan's withdrawal. Sometimes I would be active and affectionate, hoping to pull him out of it. Other times I would act as if nothing were wrong, hoping he would pull himself out of it. Frequently, I too would withdraw, hoping he would notice and do something about it. When these maneuvers didn't work, I would get angry or hurt, blaming him for our distance.

The one thing I was not willing to take the responsibility for was bringing us closer by telling him what I was feeling. It was much safer for me to blame Jordan. If I didn't take the responsibility for getting what I wanted, I would never have to risk being rejected.

I didn't want to continue blaming Jordan, and I didn't want to take all the responsibility for getting us close. I also didn't want to continue my other maneuvers.

I knew what I didn't want to do, but I certainly didn't know what I did want to do.

I Don't Trust Her

As scared as I was of Margie's being in school, I was much more frightened by her relationship with Barbara. I hated it. I'd seen Barbara spin her web before. She'd sucked me into her life once; perhaps she could do it to Margie.

Margie did not see Barbara's behavior as manipulative. As I felt Barbara pulling at Margie for more time, Margie kept reassuring me that she knew what was happening, that she didn't want anything more than the two mornings a week she was already spending, and I shouldn't worry. Our friends also became involved with Barbara, and everyone loved her. I felt even more alone in my distrust and anger.

Margie always seemed so committed to our relationship, and yet I never trusted her. Very often in our arguments she would accuse me of that, but I always denied it. How could I admit it? She was honest, forthright, and she loved me. I had no reason not to trust her, but I didn't.

The Carry-Over Of Loving

"How come you don't seem to trust how I feel about you?" I asked Jordan. "I've been so much in love with you throughout our marriage, and I've shown you in so many ways, yet when I do one thing you don't like, you're convinced that I don't care about you or that I'm going to want to leave you."

"I know you love me. I don't know why I get so anxious," Jordan said.

"Well, either you don't accept the positive feelings I send or they don't seem to carry-over from one day to the next. It's like you've got your bags packed with one foot out the door."

"You know I have fears about many things, and when I feel that a fear is going to be confirmed I'm ready to give up. So no matter how many good things happen, it takes only one bad thing to create anxiety."

I told Jordan, "It's one of the most frustrating problems in our relationship. I feel I've already proven myself to you, and yet you constantly challenge me to keep proving myself. I feel I can't act in certain ways for fear you'll take it as proof that I don't love you. It amazes and frustrates me that it's so easy for you to sweep away our years of loving in a moment of insecurity. I'd be much less guarded if I knew you trusted how I feel about you."

Little White Lies

"I'll be back in an hour." I knew it would probably be more like two hours.

When I returned home Jordan had that "look" on his face.

"How come you're so late?"

"Oh, I got involved in a discussion and I just couldn't leave."

Jordan seemed annoyed and distant, but he didn't say anything more. I played the scene many times. The little white lies usually worked.

Then one day Jordan exploded. "I can't stand this. I feel like I'm being deceived. You tell me one thing and then another thing happens. I feel like you're always trying to hide something from me."

"I am," I said. "If I tell you I'm going to be gone two hours instead of one, then I'm afraid you'll disapprove, give me your look, and withdraw. I hate it when you do that. I'll do almost anything to avoid it. If you want me to be open and honest with you, then don't respond that way to me."

"How can I guarantee that I won't be upset? I don't know whether I'm going to be happy with your honesty, but it makes me even more anxious and hurt when I think I'm not getting the whole truth."

Being honest meant that I had to take the responsibility for my actions. I had to decide for myself what I wanted, and be willing then to deal with Jordan's reaction to it. Even the Look.

Our Marriage In Turmoil

I gave Margie the look and withdrew both before and after she spent time with Barbara. Most of the time we didn't confront each other, and for days there would be distance between us. But eventually we'd get into an argument over my withdrawal and her behavior. Each time we'd resolve the argument by arriving at a new understanding. We'd come up with new ideas about what we could do to end the fights.

Good feelings resumed, and we hoped and expected the conflicts would cease. But they didn't.

My ultimate hope was that if Margie and I were miserable enough because of her relationship with Barbara, she would give it up. Nothing worked. We had more fights and unhappiness during this year than in the previous eight years of marriage combined. Each time we argued, Margie became more and more frustrated and distrustful.

It seemed as if we were always fighting over the issue of control. Margie was unhappy with our "system." I thought this must be what families go through when a teenager starts to rebel against the control of his parents. I began to wonder whether the marriage was worth all of this turmoil. I knew that we were at the point where many marriages fail. It seemed like it would be easier to start over with someone new.

Who Helps The Marriage Counselors?

It was morning and we were in the midst of another battle about Margie's relationship with Barbara. It had raged on and off for days, and we were no closer to resolving it than when we started.

I said to Margie, "We're not getting anywhere. What do you want to do?"

"Let's call Bobbie and Chet and see if they can help us."

"No, I don't want to."

Margie had suggested this on other occasions, and I always rejected the idea. Even though hundreds of couples had fought in front of us, I couldn't picture myself fighting in front of our friends. I was afraid that I would look foolish. I had always maintained a self-possessed image that people looked up to. Would they like me if they saw the side of me that didn't have it all together?

We'd been able to work out all of our conflicts by ourselves, and we would get through this one too.

We went about the day's business coldly ignoring each other. In the afternoon I tried to make contact with Margie. That blew up into another yelling match. In desperation I agreed to allow our friends to help us.

Margie called and asked if we could come to their house after we finished work at 10:30 p.m. They agreed.

We were silent as we drove to their home.

For two hours Bobbie and Chet helped us to hear each other and to clarify our own thinking. When we blamed each other, they helped us focus on what we were feeling about ourselves. They would express what they thought we might be feeling, and in this way helped us to understand each other. They didn't judge either of us, or take sides. They just helped us to know and express our feelings and to listen, really listen to each other.

Although Bobbie and Chet are not therapists, they've both had a lot of counseling experience and were able to do for us what we had done for so many couples. I realized that just because we are marriage counselors and can very effectively help others with their difficulties, doesn't necessarily mean we can always solve our own.

With the help of our friends we had taken another step toward resolving a difficult problem but, more important, we had experienced the benefits of fighting constructively in front of others.

I felt relieved as we drove home. I had shown a side of myself that I felt bad about to Bobbie and Chet, and they still liked me. In fact, they said that it was easier to like me because they felt closer to me.

It was an amazing evening. I had done a scary thing and wound up feeling good about myself. Margie and I felt very close.

I Don't Want Our System

"What's the matter?"

"Nothing."

I had to do something to deal with this situation. I decided I would ask Jordan "What's the matter?" only once, and if he responded with "nothing" it would be up to him to deal with his problems when he was ready to.

It was a solution, but it didn't work. Jordan still didn't react any differently. He just continued to withdraw, and the distance between us grew wider and wider.

I could tolerate our system no longer. It was causing me to miss out on too much—it was destroying my good feelings about myself and my loving feelings for Jordan.

As I became more certain of what I wanted and that I had a right to it, I became more and more resentful of Jordan's efforts to control me.

I realized that Jordan would not stop trying to control me just because I asked him to. He would change his behavior only if he was affected by my reaction. I was the one who was unhappy, and it was up to me to do something about it.

From then on, each time he withdrew and gave me the look, I reacted more and more angrily until one day I finally blew up.

In the past my rage had frightened me, and I had put a lid on it. But now I showed it to him. "I can't stand your silence! I feel like I'm talking to a wall! I feel like I don't even exist when you won't talk to me! I hate it and I hate you when I feel that you're trying to control me. I just want to get away from you. I can't stand the fact that you don't trust me. I'm going to start thinking more about me from now on!"

Maybe I Don't Want Our System Either

"I hate you when I feel that you're trying to control me. I just want to get away from you! I'm going to start thinking more about me from now on!"

Those words cut through me like a knife. All my fears were going to come true. She hates me, she wants to get away from me, our marriage is just about over. I was terrified. I didn't know if I could change. I didn't want to change.

· "Does this mean you aren't going to consider my feelings any more?" I asked.

"No. I love you, and your feelings are very important to me. But I want to become more aware of what I want to do in any situation and then tell you about it instead of letting you decide for me. We'll have to try to find a way both of us can get what we want."

It is only possible to control another person's behavior if that person is willing to go along with it. I had been living in constant fear of the time when Margie would not allow it anymore and now it had come.

When Margie decided she didn't want our system any longer, it forced both of us to become aware of the ways it was hurting us and our relationship.

Only when she would no longer allow me to manipulate her into doing what I wanted her to do was it possible to trust her. If I could manipulate her, others who are important would also be able to.

Only when I could accept Margie as a free person, confident in her own decisions, would I be able to believe she was not acting out of obligation or fear of my displeasure.

Only when Margie could feel my acceptance of her, which is the opposite of wanting to control and change her, could she feel fully loving toward me.

Only when she acted out of desire for me could I feel truly loved.

But becoming aware of the reasons for my behavior didn't mean that I was willing to give up control. Being in control is a powerful position.

In keeping a lid on Margie's spontaneity, I had had to keep a lid on my own. What would be the result if I were to let go?

Fighting To Resolution

Although we had come to many awarenesses in understanding our system, we needed to go through many more conflicts and discussions in order to create the kind of relationship we both wanted.

Sometimes our conflicts were quiet discussions and were over in five minutes. At other times, the battles raged for hours. We often screamed with frustration at not being understood. But we stayed with it, even though we had to interrupt the argument to work or take care of the children. We'd stay up all night rather than leave the argument unresolved.

For us, resolution means an awareness and understanding of the issues. When Jordan understands me and I understand him, the argument is over. It doesn't necessarily mean that we reach an agreement. Most of our arguments are not over facts; they are over issues for which there is not a single right answer. Therefore, understanding an issue is far more important to us than reaching an agreement. Generally, the understanding leads to acceptance, and with the acceptance, the warm feeling comes flooding back.

Sometimes, even though I understand and accept the way Jordan feels, and believe that he has a right to feel that way, I still don't like his behavior if it hurts me. But at this point, unless I want to continue to try to convince him that he should change, there's nothing more to argue about. All I can do is decide what I'm going to do when he does the thing I don't like.

Secrets
and
Revelations

I Don't Like It When People Try To Change Me

"For God's sake, just listen to me," Jordan often said to me. Sometimes that was very difficult to do.

When he wants me to help him understand his own reactions and is not trying to control or change my behavior, I find it very easy to listen and understand his pain, fear, anxiety, frustration or disappointment.

But if I feel he's attacking me or criticizing me, and demanding that I change, then I usually defend myself and refuse to listen.

When he attacks the way that I am, then I don't want to listen. Statements like "What's the matter with you?" or "How could you have done such a thing?" are direct attacks on my integrity. They imply that there's something wrong with me. I resent it when someone else implies that they know what's the right thing for me to feel or to do.

If Jordan says to me, "I hate it when you come rushing in just before we have to start work. I like to spend a few minutes talking about our day first," I'm far more likely to change my behavior than if he attacks me with "What's the matter with you? You're always rushing in at the last minute!"

I may change my behavior in order to win approval from another, but that way is never as satisfactory as changing as a result of my own awareness. Then I don't resent anyone, and I feel really good about me.

You Can't Make Me Talk,
You Can Help Me Want To

"I want more from you, Jordan. I need you to tell me more about how you feel."

I heard this in one form or another for years. Most of the time I truly didn't know what I felt.

I had good reasons for keeping myself in ignorance. Because I believed that what I felt was often not "acceptable" to Margie, myself, or anyone else, I didn't want to let her or even myself in on my feelings.

On the other hand, when I began to realize that Margie accepted what I am and how I feel, I became willing to reveal myself.

It's impossible for either of us to be accepting of the other if we believe there is a right way to be or a right way to feel. If Margie says to me, "You have no reason to feel that way," or "It's unhealthy to feel that way," or "It's wrong to feel that way," then I am not being respected. If on the other hand she says, "I can understand why you feel that way because . . ." or "I don't understand why you feel that way, but you must have many good reasons and I'd like to understand what they are," then I feel accepted and I'm willing to explore myself.

Ways To Control

As Jordan gave up his attempts to control me, I wanted to spend more time with him. I no longer felt anxious about saying something that would cause him to withdraw.

"I want to confess," he said to me one day, "that I really haven't trusted you all this time. I knew that if I could control you, so could Barbara. Now that you're not letting me do it, I'm no longer worried about your relationship with her."

His statement shocked me as I realized how right he'd been. As I looked back, I saw that I'd done many of the same things with her that I'd done with Jordan—little lies to avoid her anger and withdrawal, and not reacting honestly to her attempts to control me.

In dealing with our system and in our counseling, Jordan and I have become aware of the many ways in which people attempt to control each other. Control, to us, is when someone communicates to another that he should change what he thinks, feels, says or does, and that if he doesn't, he will be punished in some way.

The attempt to control says, "There is something wrong with the way you are and you should change."

When criticism, anger and withdrawal are intended to create guilt or fear, they are attempts to control. Threats of withholding love, of ending a relationship, of withdrawing financial support, of physical violence, of becoming ill, or attempting suicide are more blatant efforts to control. Even a tone of voice or a facial expression that intimates "you are doing something or you have done something wrong" is a device for control.

When one person attempts to control another, whether or not the person succeeds, the attempt usually alienates the other person. No one likes to be punished or made to feel bad about the way he is or the way he feels.

Little Secrets Build Big Walls

It's the first time I've let myself feel sexually attracted to another man since we've been married. I wonder if I should tell Jordan? I wonder how he'll react? If I don't tell him, he'll never find out and I won't have to deal with it. On the other hand, I'm confused about how to handle these turned-on feelings, and I want to talk with him about it. I don't want to act on these feelings, but they scare me. I really want to talk to Jordan. But maybe he'll be too hurt or scared to listen. If he gets angry, then we'll end up in a fight. I wish I knew what to do.

If I decide not to tell Jordan about something I've felt or done, then that area becomes closed to discussion and discovery. The more secrets I keep, the more areas are closed. Each time I close off an area, I build a wall between us. The more secrets, the thicker the wall.

At times I believed that Jordan was too fragile to hear what I'd done or felt, and that our relationship would be damaged if I told him. I preferred the wall to what I imagined would be disastrous consequences. But when I judged the time to be right, I'd tell him my secret and the wall would come down.

If I have the freedom to discuss my sexual feelings for others with Jordan, we can discover why I have them, what's missing with us. If I can't discuss them, chances are at some time I will act on them. If I decide to act on them and can't tell Jordan, then the wall just gets thicker.

Each time I've told Jordan things that I thought would scare him or make him angry, I've been glad that I did. We've gotten into many arguments over what I've told him, but the result has always been closer, more intimate feelings between us.

But I still wait for the "right" time—a time when I think there's a good chance that he'll really listen and not judge me.

Feelings Are Intentional

"You seem depressed," Jordan said.

"Yeah, I am."

"How come?"

"I don't know. This day's been such a hassle, I guess it just got me down."

We were lying on our bed, taking a late-afternoon breather. I began to think about the depressed feelings that had just descended on me.

"You know," I finally said to Jordan, "although I hate to admit it, these down feelings are intentional. I want to be depressed because then maybe no one will make demands on me. When I'm overwhelmed by your demands or the children's, I feel down in the hope that everyone will leave me alone."

"Why don't you just tell us to leave you alone?"

"Because I feel I should want to meet the demands. I'm afraid if I say I don't want to, you'll all be disappointed or angry. But if I'm obviously depressed you'll leave me alone without my having to ask."

"It works pretty well, doesn't it? When you're down, it's like wearing a sign saying 'stay away!'"

Most of the time it seems like my feelings just happen to me. But if I admit that how I feel has to do with what I feel about myself in relation to others, then I have to take responsibility for my feelings.

I can't just change my feelings, but if I'm unhappy about them, I can explore how I choose to see myself.

Honesty Is Self-Revelation

"That was a difficult session," Margie said. "Those people are so intent on being what they call honest that they're destroying their marriage."

"Yeah, almost every sentence out of Al's mouth was 'Here's what's wrong with you,' and when Cindy objected or defended herself, Al came back with, 'Well, after all, you know it's the truth. I'm only being honest.'"

"It was amazing. They never revealed anything about themselves, but they sure knew exactly what was wrong with the other person. When he told her she was too long-waisted to be attractive, I couldn't believe it. What can she do about being long-waisted? We'll have to help him focus on what he hopes to gain by that kind of honesty. It certainly doesn't help them understand each other."

For Margie and me honesty means "Here's how I feel," rather than telling the other person what's wrong with him or pumping another's feelings without revealing our own.

"You're a bitch" says nothing specific about what I feel. The response is bound to be defensive. A more honest reaction might be, "Goddammit, I can't stand all your complaining. I'm so irritated I just want to leave!"

"It scares me when you threaten to hit me" is far more revealing than "You're a bully."

"I lose interest when you talk about business all the time" is more honest than "You're a bore."

"I want to make love" is far more revealing than "How do you feel tonight?"

"I'd like to go to a movie" is more honest than "What do you want to do later?"

The intimacy of our relationship is directly proportional to our willingness to be honest about ourselves.

Understanding "Irrational" Behavior

"Slow down! Don't go so fast!" I clutched the seat and Jordan's leg.

"Look, I'm a good driver and I'm only going thirty miles an hour. Relax, there's nothing to worry about."

"But I'm scared."

Mountain roads terrified me. It was a constant battle. In my terror, I'd yell at Jordan to slow down. In his irritation he would tell me to leave him alone and lecture me about being so irrational.

One day Jordan asked me, "What happens to you on those roads?"

"Every time we come to a curve, I imagine the car going off the cliff."

"Really? I wonder why that happens to you?"

We spent a long time talking about it. I explored the past, when I first felt the fear and what's happened since.

Finally I said, "And when you get mad at me, it makes me even more afraid."

"But it's so hard to accept behavior that I consider to be irrational. It's so frustrating when you do something I don't understand," Jordan said. "I think, 'It's stupid for her to feel that way. She should be able to do something about it.' I get angry when you don't."

I'd never before let Jordan in on the feelings behind my supposedly "irrational" behavior. When I finally did, he was able to understand, and tolerate it.

"Now, slow down, okay?"

"Okay."

She Doesn't Think Like I Do

It was a beautiful Sunday morning. The children were playing quietly in the den. We were in bed cuddling as the sun bathed our naked bodies. I could have stayed like that for hours.

Margie's voice jolted me. "It's time to get up. We've got to be at USC by ten for my workshop."

"Fuck the workshop! Why can't we just stay here and enjoy this moment?"

"I want to go to the workshop," she said.

I was angry. "We spent all day yesterday at that workshop, and it was a boring waste of time."

"I know," she said, "but maybe today it will be better."

"You'd rather go to the workshop than stay here?"

"Yes."

"Well, I'm not going to go." If she preferred the workshop to me, that was her choice. I moved away from her and pulled the cover up.

Margie got dressed in silence and left for USC. I spent the day at home with the children.

At four o'clock when Margie walked in, I searched her face to see if she was still upset. I said, "How was the workshop?"

"It was much better today. He changed the way he presented the material, and we all got a lot more out of it." She was distant and reserved, and I didn't care about her answer.

"Why are you so afraid to miss anything?"

"I don't think I'm afraid I'll miss something, but when I make a commitment to something, I want to follow through on it. I signed up for a weekend workshop, and that's where all my thoughts were directed."

"You know, that's really different from the way I approach things. I'm always ready to change my plans if I see a way out of a difficult or unpleasant situation."

I saw that Margie's behavior was not a rejection of me. If she had seen the same options that I did and then had chosen to go to the workshop, she would have been choosing the workshop over me. But since she never even recognized the options once she had committed herself, it was not a choice and I was not rejected.

I wonder how often I've made that mistake before.

At The Mercy Of My Hormones

The week before my menstrual period has always been a hard time for me. I'm restless, irritable, and nervous. I'm less tolerant of mistakes in myself and others. Things that I normally don't notice irritate me and make me angry. I cry easily.

I feel resentful and helpless that something out of my control is making life more difficult for me and for everyone around me.

I have always wanted Jordan's understanding and help during these times, but this has been hard for him. He has trouble believing that I am so affected by my period, since he's not riding this kind of hormonal roller coaster. But when he puts his arms around me, reminding me to take it easy, and that things aren't really as bad as they seem, it somehow makes it easier for me.

Every month I say to myself, "Next month I won't let myself fly off the handle. I can have control over it." But every month I realize that I am at the mercy of my hormones, and I am grateful for Jordan's understanding.

Expectations Are Setups For Disaster

"It sure would be nice to have some time for myself," Margie said wistfully.

"Maybe I could change some of my commitments around so that I could take Sheryl out one morning a week. You could have the house all to yourself." Margie's face lit up.

Our morning outing was lovely for both Sheryl and me, and I returned home feeling really good. Margie was sunning in our backyard, reading a book. I greeted her with a "Hi" and a kiss. She just mumbled, "I'd like to finish this chapter."

I waited for something more from her. Nothing came, so I went into the house. I felt like hell.

She came in after a while, sensed that something was wrong, and we went through a "What's the Matter?"—"Nothing" routine.

I finally blew up. "You don't appreciate the things I do to make your life more pleasant."

"I do appreciate your efforts," she yelled, "but I was deeply involved in my book. What did you expect me to do, leap up and hug you?"

That last sentence touched something in me. "Yeah, I did. I had a fantasy of you being so grateful to me that you'd throw your arms around me, thank me for taking Sheryl, and tell me what a neat morning you'd had."

We calmed down. I realized I often fantasize about how Margie will respond to what I'm going to do. I thought about how often I'd been disappointed when my fantasies didn't come true. When this happened, I usually got angry at Margie because she hadn't acted the way I'd expected her to.

But Margie had no way of knowing what I expected. My disappointment was the result of my expectations not being fulfilled. When I took responsibility for setting up the situation, then I could feel my disappointment without being angry at her.

I could also have taken the responsibility to get what I wanted rather than just wait and hope for her response. That morning I could have said, "Hi, how did you enjoy spending two hours alone?" or "How was your nice quiet morning?" and I would have gotten my appreciation.

I hope I can remember to do it.

Always The Nice Guy

"I just know that that mechanic really screwed me and I just smiled and said, 'Thank you.' I sure do wind up feeling bad about myself when people take advantage of me and I don't do anything about it. Yet it keeps happening. I just don't understand it."

I come from a long line of nice guys; easygoing, quiet, always willing to help a friend. We don't argue, we give in to avoid a conflict, we don't voice strong opinions or make demands. Everyone likes us. No one knows us.

I learned early to be a good boy. My mother boasted that when I was three years old she could put a clean white suit on me and it would stay clean all day long. A good boy who grew up to be a nice guy.

To accomplish this, I had to give up openly expressing what I felt and wanted and just say yes to whatever others wanted. If I had strong feelings and fought for them, people might be angry with me and not want to have me around. If I had strong needs and made them known, people might resent me. If I knew what I wanted and went after it, I'd have to take responsibility for the consequences of my actions. It was far easier and less risky to be a nice guy.

"You give up a lot to maintain a nice-guy image," Margie said to me.

"I get a lot from it also."

"I'm sure you do, but it has an effect on how I feel about you. I always love you, but when you're feeling good about yourself, you come across very differently. You're more confident, outgoing, humorous, and open. I feel so good about you when you're that way that I can't keep my hands off you."

"I like myself better too. I feel really strong at those times. And the strange thing about it is that the conflicts which I dread so much usually don't happen, and when they do, they're really not all that bad. I sure would like to be more assertive and outgoing. It would be breaking a long-standing tradition in my family, but it's worth a try."

Giving up being a nice guy doesn't mean that I have become a bastard, running over everyone's feelings. I am still concerned with others, but the pain of being a nice guy has become too great.

When I smile in agreement even though I don't mean it, I feel bad about myself. To deny my right to my feelings is to deny myself. To mold myself into what others want me to be kills the spontaneity that makes me me.

To have everyone like me, I must give up something important—me.

A New System

My worst fears have not come true. Change has not ended our relationship or even weakened it.

If only one of us had changed, our marriage would surely have ended. But we were willing to engage in the conflicts and struggle through the changes that every new awareness brought. We have become happier and our relationship stronger because we have confronted and understood many difficult areas within ourselves.

As we discover new things about ourselves and about each other, we feel the intense excitement of intimacy.

If we had separated because of our problems, we would never have had to face and work through the issues surrounding control and freedom, which are basic to how we relate with each other. If we had split up and started new relationships, eventually we would have come to the same place and found the same issues.

As with all the other major changes in our lives, we were reluctant to change our safe, comfortable ways of behaving even when that behavior made us unhappy. It's only as we gained awareness of the good reasons we had for doing what we were doing, and of how unhappy it made us, that change took place.

Our new system means that we each take full responsibility for the fact that we are free to know what we want and go after it. We are willing to work through the consequences of our decisions. Neither of us has ever functioned this way before. We are growing into it slowly.

Our new system is unpredictable and potentially difficult. But when we look back and allow ourselves to feel again the full weight of the doubts and insecurities created by the old system, we realize that we have made the right choice.

The future is frightening. The present is exciting.

Affirmations and Freedom

Celebrations

Mother's Day 1974. I wanted to be celebrated. I wanted Jordan to slip quietly out of bed and do a whole Mother's Day number with the kids. That morning I lay in bed waiting for Jordan to do something special. He didn't.

I had never told him how I felt about being celebrated. All through our marriage he had put down holidays—birthdays, Valentine's Day, Mother's Day, and special occasions. He called them phony and commercial. I didn't feel about holidays the way he did, but knowing how he felt, it would have been embarrassing to say, "I would like you to make a big fuss over me on Mother's Day."

I decided right then and there to tell Jordan how I remembered Mother's Day when I was a kid. "I would spend a long time making a card and making a present. I loved surprising my mother. My father and I would make a special breakfast for her. Sometimes we'd make a whole day of it. I would get into the spirit of giving and the excitement of her excitement. Our children never do that for me, and I have the feeling they don't because you put it down. I feel sad about that."

As I shared my feelings and started to feel a little better, I looked at Jordan. He was in tears. "What's the matter?"

"I'm just remembering what Mother's Day meant to me," he said. "My mother wanted to be celebrated, but I was often angry and resentful toward her. Same thing on other occasions, especially anniversaries. My parents were obviously unhappy with each other, and yet I felt obliged to celebrate their marriage. Celebrations were so phony."

His negative feelings about holidays had carried over from his childhood and had prevented us from experiencing the joys of celebration.

The awareness of what we wanted now and of what had kept us from it finally brought us back to good feelings. Jordan got out of bed, got the children together, and said, "Let's all celebrate Mommy." I almost started to cry. I loved it.

I'm looking forward to my birthday, Valentine's Day, Mother's Day, Christmas, Hanukkah, and even Chinese New Year's.

Good Feelings Are Impossible
If Perfection Is Necessary

"My breasts sag, my stomach is full of stretch marks and I have a broad ass. I hate my body."

One of the youngest and most attractive members of my women's group was talking. We were sharing our feelings about our bodies and she was the first to speak up.

"Well, my breasts are too small," said another.

"And my thighs are too big."

"The skin on my ass puckers."

And so it went around the room, each one of us embarrassed about some part of her body.

"As a teenager I rarely saw other girls nude and so had no opportunity to compare my body with theirs and decide if mine was okay," I said. "My only models were sex queens like Marilyn Monroe. As I look back, I probably had a beautiful body, but I couldn't love it. It just didn't look perfect.

"When Jordan and I got married, the centerfold of *Playboy* was the ideal. I didn't measure up then and after having babies and getting stretch marks, I really felt bad. But Jordan has always loved seeing me nude, and he can't keep his hands off. He helped me to feel okay about my body."

We continued to discuss our concerns. I suggested that we take off our clothes. We shared our anxieties about being seen nude by each other, and then agreed to try it.

"Your breasts are beautiful," someone said to me. I was shocked. Jordan had always told me they were beautiful, but I had never believed him.

As I looked around, I realized that my body looked pretty good. And so did everyone else's. Not perfect but pretty good—and that's enough.

Nobody Ever Told Me That Before

I was shaving nude when Margie came in and started to run her hands over my body. "I love your body," she said.

"You do?"

"Yes, I love to look at you."

"How come you never said that to me before?"

"I don't know. It's obvious that you have a nice body. I guess I was embarrassed to say it."

"But I've never felt good about my body. My chest is too thin, and I'm not muscular enough."

"I've never liked men with super-muscular builds."

"I thought girls were attracted to the Charles Atlas type."

"Maybe some girls are, but most of the women I know aren't."

I knew Margie didn't dislike my body, but to hear that she loved it made me feel terrific. I looked in the mirror. It really was nice. I wanted to hear more. "What else do you like about my body?" I asked.

"I love your soft, smooth skin and your delicate hands."

"Yeah, they are delicate, never having done a hard day's work in their lives."

"I love your penis." She started to fondle it.

"Well, I like it too when it's erect, but it seems so small when it's not erect. I've felt bad all my life because my penis is so small."

"You have a beautiful penis and I love its size. What difference does it make what size it is when it's not erect?"

"None, I guess, but I've always felt that anyone who saw my non-erect penis would secretly laugh at me. When I see men with bigger penises I envy them. I know what I've read, but don't women really want a man to have a really large penis? The bigger the better?"

"That's not the way I feel. My feelings during intercourse are tied up with how I feel about you."

"The fact that you love my body so is incredible to me."

I felt super.

What Have I Been Missing All These Years?

For many years, it had never occurred to me to think of men's bodies, especially their genitals, as beautiful and arousing.

As I was growing up, it was women's bodies that were portrayed as beautiful and sexual. Nude women were on calendars and in magazines. Women were in the beauty contests. Women's measurements were published.

Through my women's groups I discovered that a few very sexual women were highly aroused by the sight of their man's nude body and especially by his penis. I realized that if I allowed myself, I could become as excited by Jordan's body as he was by mine.

I began to notice the contours of his muscles, the distribution of hair on his body, the texture of his skin in contrast to the texture of his hair.

Above all, I began to pay attention to his penis. How was it I had never really seen it before? I became fascinated with the way it hung and moved when he walked around naked. I loved the way it shriveled up when it got cold, and poked out again when it warmed up. I marveled at the softness of its tip and at the hardness of its erection. I admired the beauty of its upward curve. I discovered the sensuality of his testicles, and the smoothness at the base of his scrotum.

I can love his body as he loves mine.

Giving Compliments Is Important

"I loved your telling me your feelings about my body," I told Margie. "I wish you'd tell me more often about things you like."

"I don't know why, but it's hard for me to give you a lot of compliments," Margie replied. "For some reason it seems so much easier to tell you about the things that I don't like than it is to say the things I really appreciate about you. Lots of times I feel good things about you, but I just don't say them."

"You let me know how you feel about me when we make love, but I need to know other times as well. I think that if I had an affair, it would be because I was getting those good feelings of being appreciated rather than for sex."

Hearing what Margie loves about me is very important to me. When I feel appreciated by her, I love being with her—especially when she compliments not just the things that I've done or accomplished, but me, the way I am.

Accepting Compliments Is Hard

"If you like to hear positive things so much, how come you get so embarrassed when I tell you what I love about you?" Margie was half-joking, half-serious.

"I don't know. I love to hear it, but it makes me feel uncomfortable. It's as if I'm not supposed to admit that I'm good. It's probably the same reason I would have trouble bragging about myself. I remember being told that other people wouldn't like me if I was too cocky."

"When I give you a compliment and you don't seem to appreciate it, I feel dumb and I sure don't want to put myself in that position very often."

"Okay, I promise that I'll accept your compliments more easily."

"You're terrific."

"That's true."

Not So Fragile

I spent a great deal of my life in a prison, a self-imposed prison.

I was willing to sacrifice my happiness in the present to protect myself from any future potential unhappiness.

I believed I was fragile, that I couldn't take it if I were hurt emotionally. I was never sure what "take it" meant but I didn't want to find out. When I finally confronted myself with myself, I discovered that I have in fact withstood a great deal of emotional pain. In my past relationships I've often been rejected. But as devastated as I felt during those times, I have survived. I have been terribly disappointed in myself and others. Still I have bounced back. In reality, I don't fall apart.

As an independent person, Margie might do things that would hurt me, frighten me, or embarrass me, but I would not be destroyed personally and our marriage would not end. Whatever happened we would discuss it, understand it, work it out, and grow as a result.

As I saw my vulnerability as a myth, I could also identify it as another controlling device. As long as Margie believed that I was fragile, she would act to protect me.

Now when I allow myself to react to things around me, my feelings are intensified, and although I feel my hurt, fear or pain I am also more open to the joys of life. If I'm flying high and something brings me down, the crash is painful, humiliating, and depressing.

I don't want to feel those lows. But in order to live fully, I need to accept that there's nothing wrong with me for wanting to protect myself from potentially hurtful situations, but I also need to remember that when I get hurt, I can survive the pain.

Cutting out the highs in my life takes away most of the joy. I've tired of my prison. I want to live.

Kids Have All The Fun: I Want Some

"I'd like to have more fun together," I told Margie.

"Why do you say that?"

"Well, I started thinking about it today while I was at the park with Sheryl. I noticed that most of the adults were just sitting there, lost in their own thoughts. I imagined that they were thinking about what they'd rather be doing or that they were caught up in the responsibility of their children.

"The children were yelling and screaming and running and falling and laughing and crying. They were alive and intense. Sheryl laughed and said, 'Let's run, Daddy.' We ran together and she loved it. I felt suddenly free with her, like a kid, and I started to laugh. I felt my whole body moving and the wind on my face, and my hair bouncing and my heart pounding and the grass on my feet. She threw herself on the grass and I fell next to her. We rolled, laughing and hugging. I felt happy and close to her.

"Then I started thinking that I'd like for the two of us to have more of that kind of fun."

Our children almost always have it. Eric laughs with his whole body, literally consumed with his joy. Josh plays at the water's edge and when a wave knocks him over he comes up jumping with uncontrollable excitement. Sheryl feels the sound and rhythm of music in her two-year-old body and responds with spontaneous movement.

"It's so much easier to be that way when we're with them," I said.

"Well, they're kids and it's easier to be a kid with them. I can't imagine just messing around with you all that spontaneously. That's what I used to do in high school or when we met. Somehow it doesn't fit my image of a father or a mother," Margie said.

"I know exactly what you mean. I've got the same image."

We had great times as lovers. We were carefree. Then marriage, a career, children, a house—each one added a weight to our existence. We became serious and responsible, and the weight of our responsibilities became more and more oppressive.

"We've been missing out on a whole dimension of our lives!"

"Yeah, I'd really like to play more with you."

"Let's do it!"

Gotta Dance, Gotta Dance

We finally bought that new stereo.

Jordan set up the speakers in our living room and bedroom, and our house filled with music.

That evening we put on an album and started to dance. It was an exhilarating experience. We had a feeling of freedom as we allowed our bodies to move spontaneously to the sounds and rhythms.

We watched each other's bodies move. We got warm from our dancing and removed our clothes. As we danced we looked and touched, held and kissed each other and experienced the sensual delight of dancing nude. Our sex that evening was a loving and passionate experience. Music played an important part in our lovemaking. The sounds and rhythms affected our mood and movements. They added to the spontaneity of the experience.

Music has added new dimensions to our lives. Instead of walking through the house, we sometimes dance from room to room. Occasionally we pass each other and stop to spend a few minutes dancing together.

The World Is Our Playground

I have tasted freedom.

Playing at the beach, at home, in a restaurant. Dancing around the house. Almost any place can be our playground.

When I'm feeling free, I react to everything around me. I feel things intensely—people, the sunset, the ocean on my feet. Sounds need to come out of my body. When I laugh, it comes from by belly instead of my throat. When I stop worrying about how I'm coming across and just react, I find humor everywhere.

My voice is not level and controlled. My body is not stiff and tense. I am loose and expressive. I am on a natural high.

I really see Margie. I notice the subtleties in her face and body, and I respond to her unique beauty. I feel intensely loving when I stop worrying about myself and allow her presence to penetrate me.

We are closest and happiest when we are able to let go and respond to each other. Sharing our play and our laughter is a very intimate experience. Our relationship is never routine or boring when we react spontaneously to each other. We walk down the street holding hands, our arms swinging and a smile on our faces. Adding the dimension of shared fun has given our relationship a feeling of wholeness.

My arm-swinging, free-wheeling feelings come and go. I still pull in and withdraw sometimes when I'm upset or scared. Spontaneity doesn't happen enough. I want more. When I'm free, I feel alive and I love everything and everybody—especially me.

Love
and
Intimacy

If We Were Both The Same

"They're so different. Their marriage will never last," people said.

Our differences have caused us many problems and at times we've wanted the other person to be just like us. But our differences have been our lifeline, an opportunity to see into another way of being.

If we were both relaxed and patient, not much would get done.

If we were both achievement oriented, we'd never relax long enough to just see or enjoy each other.

If we both moved slowly, we'd drag through life.

If we both moved fast, we'd race through life.

If we both avoided conflict, our marriage would be uninvolved, distant, and boring.

If we both felt intellectually inadequate, neither could help the other to feel okay.

If we both felt socially inadequate, we'd avoid social situations.

If we both were always serious, our marriage wouldn't be any fun.

The differences have taught us to value the unique qualities in ourselves and in each other. As a result, we've each pulled the other more into our worlds. And as we have been forced to question many things about ourselves, we have become more aware and trusting of ourselves as individuals.

Doorways To Intimacy

Almost any experience we have together can take us to a doorway to intimacy, but passing through that doorway takes one-to-one intense time. That comes only when we are emotionally available to ourselves and each other.

A vacation is a doorway to intimacy. We pass through when we put away the clocks and listen to our bodies— sleeping when we're tired, eating when we're hungry, and making love any time we want. We go with the moment and stay in the moment.

Reading is a doorway. Sharing our reactions creates the intimacy.

Humor is a doorway. Sharing our laughter and silliness and fun moves us closer together.

Dreams and fantasies are doorways. Telling our most private worlds helps us know ourselves and our relationship.

Having positive feelings about Margie is a doorway. When I tell her about them, intimate feelings grow.

Conflict, too, is a doorway. When we fight openly, listening to each other and exposing ourselves, we emerge with intensely intimate feelings.

Bedtime is a doorway. Intimacy occurs when we hold each other's warm naked body and share our thoughts.

Making love is a doorway. But only when we combine our sexual feelings with other loving feelings does our sexual experience create intense intimacy between us.

Merely spending time together isn't enough. Sometimes Margie and I spend lots of time together and don't experience the excitement of intimacy. If one of us is walled off from the other, then we could make love for hours, or talk endlessly into the night, or read a million books together and we wouldn't be any closer to each other.

Intimacy Is Scary

Committed intimacy is risky and terrifying, because there's always the possibility of loss.

Early in our marriage I came to an important realization about intimacy and loving: Whatever happens, I can survive.

If a catastrophe happened to a person I love, or to that person's love for me, I would not kill myself, go crazy, or give up my zest for life.

This realization has allowed me to take the risk and open myself up to Jordan and to my children, or to anyone else I choose to be intimate with. This doesn't mean that I'm never scared about losing them. On the contrary, I occasionally fantasize awful things happening—Jordan in a car accident, a child becoming seriously ill—and I'm terrified. They mean so much to me that the thought of losing them is excruciating.

But intimacy is worth it. It's worth whatever pain I may have to endure in the future to have a complete and intimate relationship now.

The more I open myself to Jordan by letting him know my thoughts and feelings, the more special and irreplaceable he becomes. I have a picture in my mind of what it means to me to love and be intimate with someone. As I get to know them and open myself up to them, they gradually fill up a space within by body. As we become more and more intimate, the space becomes larger; it becomes unique.

Each person has his own space, and each space has its own shape and characteristics. If I were to lose that person, the space would remain forever empty. The space is unique; no one else could ever fill it. New spaces could be created, but the old one would always remain empty.

If one loses a child, one may have other children, but the space created by that child could never be filled by another. And there would be no way out of the pain. It will eventually diminish, but it will never go away.

That's what is scary about love and intimacy. They are so permanent and so risky. If I never love, never become intimate, then I never risk deep hurt.

But I have chosen to take the risks, especially with Jordan. He is so important to me. No one can ever replace him.

To me, the risks are worth it. The moments of intimacy are the heights of my life. I will never give up the extreme highs for fear of the extreme lows. The lows frighten me terribly, but the highs are what my living is all about.

Commitment

"Sometimes I get the feeling that there's nothing I could do that would make you stop loving me," Jordan said to me recently.

"Well, if you constantly made me feel bad about myself, I'd probably not feel very loving toward you. But since we've been married, I've never doubted my love for you."

"That's hard for me to believe, yet I see it's true. For most of our marriage, until recently, I've been waiting for you to find something out about me that would stop you from loving me. When you first felt that I wasn't intellectually stimulating enough for you, I thought that was the end. When you wanted longer intercourse, I was afraid you'd find someone else who was more exciting to you. When we fought over control and you became aware of how I tried to manipulate you, I thought for sure you wouldn't love me anymore. But when you stayed with it month after month until we began to understand and work it out, I realized that nothing could kill your love."

"And you've been afraid of that all these years? I should have told you sooner."

"You did really. When I think of all the problems and hassles you're willing to go through in order to get what you want with me, then I should know you'll never leave."

"I believe there's always a way to work things out between us and that allows me to commit myself fully to you. I believe strongly that once I love a person, I will love him forever."

I Need Her

I need her.

But sometimes I don't want to need her. It's been hard to accept the fact that I need things from a woman.

Sometimes I don't want to need her. If I need her then I cannot leave her.

Sometimes I don't want to need her. If I allow myself to need her, then I will depend on her and open myself to disappointment.

Sometimes I don't want to need her. When I have needs, I am vulnerable. If I need something that she doesn't need, I can be hurt by her rejection of me.

What do I really need her for? When it comes right down to it, just about anyone can meet many of my needs. I could hire someone to cook for me, clean for me, and even to have sex with.

I need her to know me and care about me.

I need her to experience all of me, even what I believe are my shortcomings, craziness, and difficulties, and to care enough to understand and accept me.

I need her to care about me enough to give me genuine comfort, support, and encouragement.

I need her to need what I alone can give to her.

I need her to share our loving sexual experiences.

I need her to be a partner in the responsibility of raising our children.

I need her to share myself with so that I don't feel alone.

I need her to be my friend.

When I need her, she becomes irreplaceable.

I need her and it's scary.

I Need Him

I need him.

Sometimes I don't want to need him. If I need him, then he has power over me and can hurt me.

Sometimes I don't want to need him. If I need him, then I may want his approval and feel bad when I don't get it.

Sometimes I don't want to need him. If I need him, then I may feel trapped by my needing because I don't want to leave him.

Sometimes I don't want to need him. If I really let myself need him, then the loss of him becomes terrifying.

Sometimes I don't want to need him. If I need him, then my freedom is altered by that need.

Sometimes I don't want to need him. If I need him to listen to me and he's angry or withdrawn, then I'm frustrated and hurt.

Sometimes I don't want to need him. To need him is to be vulnerable, and that's the scariest of all.

What do I really need him for? When it comes right down to it, just about anyone can meet many of my needs. I'm capable of supporting myself. A therapist can listen to me, and sexual partners aren't hard to find.

I need him to value what I am.

I need him to listen to me and understand what I say to him.

I need his warmth, comfort, support, and affection.

I need him to share his thoughts and feelings so that I can know him more fully.

I need him to be sensitive to me when we make love.

I need him to help make our home into a warm and loving place.

I need the special humor he brings to me.

I need him to help me when I'm having trouble dealing with the children.

I need him to help me have good feelings about myself by loving me and wanting me.

I need him to give my life and my accomplishments special meaning.

It scares me to need what only he can give me.

I Love You

I often tell you that I love you, but today I want to tell you some of the reasons why.

I love your willingness to be there for me when I'm feeling hurt or scared. When you laugh at my jokes, enjoy my singing and praise my dancing, I feel special.

I love you because your nose wrinkles up when you smile. I love the smile that lights up your face and my life. And when you laugh you infect me with your joy.

I love your interest, your enthusiasm, your intensity. Your intense desire to learn and understand as much as you can helps keep our relationship exciting. I respond to the intensity of your sexual response. Your intense joy helps keep us alive. Your intense anger . . . well, I can't say I like it, but I wouldn't want you any other way than you are.

"I love you" just doesn't say enough about how I really feel about you. I love you, and I fall in love with you again and again.

I Love You

Today I said to you, "I love you."

Later on, after you'd gone, I thought about how differently I feel about you now as compared to last year, or two years ago, or eleven years ago when we told each other "I love you" for the first time. My love does not remain constant but changes according to what goes on between us. My feelings are so much greater, more intense and complete today. So much has gone on between us that I am amazed at the process that has built our intimacy. It seems unreal to look back and find so many ways we have grown.

The areas to explore between us must be limitless, and therefore the intensity and depth of my feelings for you must be limitless.

Tomorrow when I say, "I love you," it will have a new and different meaning.

AFTERWORD

As we look back on our nineteen years together, we discover that we have lived through three different marriages. The first eight years are characterized by the many issues we confronted and resolved. During this time, however, we never really dealt with the subtle power struggles that were eroding our relationship.

In our ninth year, things started to fall apart and for the next two years, we endured a living hell. Our battles seemed endless. As quickly as we made up, we were at each other's throat again. We tried every "curative" technique we had learned in our training as therapists and even went into therapy ourselves; nothing seemed to help. The constant battling and endless talking lasted long into many nights during that period, until things finally started to improve. We focused on our issues of control and compliance and as each of us came to understand more about ourselves and each other, our relationship began to change for the better. We knew we were over the worst times but didn't yet have a clear idea of the specific process we were using to accomplish this renewed feeling of intimacy. It was at this point we decided to write *Free to Love.*

The third phase of our marriage has spanned the past nine years — years filled with deep explorations, passionate intimacy, some lows, and more and more high times. The explorations during this phase of our marriage have been unlike anything either of us had experienced before. As the barriers we had each erected to protect ourselves from our deepest fears — primarily fears of domination and disapproval —slowly crumbled, we began to understand ourselves and each other on deeper and deeper levels. As we explored, old hurts, wounds and fears were healed, putting to rest most of our on-going conflicts.

Earlier in our marriage, the intensity, intimacy and sexuality were generated primarily by conflict, fighting and then making up. But as more and more of our conflicts have been permanently resolved, we discovered we can generate the same degree of passion and intimacy through fun, laughter, play and deep explorations that occur spontaneously, rather than as a result of conflict. In the process of these explorations and discoveries, an entirely new theory about relationships has emerged. This theory, including ideas about how and why relationships fail or succeed and the communication process that can turn a conflict into a positive experience, is the subject of our second book, *Do I Have To Give Up Me To Be Loved By You?* (CompCare Publications, 1983).

The task of maintaining a loving relationship is a difficult one. People usually enter relationships with many misconceptions and fears which frustrate the search for love and intimacy; additionally, adequate models and information to overcome difficulties are scarce. Our hope is that through our sharing with you and your sharing with each other, we can all move closer to experiencing the joy that is possible from our relationships.

Jordan and Margaret Paul
January, 1983